PRACTISING ANGELS:

A CONTEMPORARY ANTHOLOGY
OF SAN FRANCISCO BAY AREA POETRY

Edited by
Michael Mayo

Seismograph Publications
San Francisco
1986

Copyrights for individual poems appear on the Acknowledgments page.

Heartfelt thanks to my friends who assisted in the preparation of this manuscript: Joel Singer, Robert Anbian, Laura Feldman, Richard Loranger, Mark Cormier, Jack Mueller, James Broughton, Rob Goldstein and David Brown. And to Jerry Ratch for the title of this collection, from his book, *Puppet* X.

Typeset at Richard Zybert Graphics by Patrick Henderson.
Cover Design by Hal Hershey.
Printed by Braun-Brumfield.

ISBN: 0-932977-31-6

Library of Congress Catalog Number: 86-060764

Published by Seismograph Publications
P.O. Box 882664
San Francisco, CA 94188

Distributed by The Subterranean Company
P.O. Box 10233
Eugene, OR 97440

TO
LEA TAMMI

&
TO
MY BROTHERS
WHO ARE ILL WITH AIDS

ACKNOWLEDGMENTS

The editor acknowledges permission from the following poets and publishers to reprint copyrighted work:

STEVE ABBOTT: "Walking This Abandoned Field," and "After Reading Catullus," from *Wrecked Hearts*, copyright © 1978 by Stephen E. Abbott, by permission of the author.

FRANCISCO X. ALARCÓN: "Prayer," "Roots," and "Wounded Words," from *Tattoos*, copyright © 1985 by Francisco X. Alarcón. "Fugitive," from *Ya Vas, Carnal*, copyright © 1985 by Humanizarte Publications. Poems by permission of the author.

FERNANDO ALEGRÍA: "The Disappeared Will Inherit the Earth," appeared in *Alcatraz, an assemblage*, copyright © 1979 by Stephen Kessler. "Elegy for Orlando Letelier," and "Nocturne," from *Changing Centuries*, copyright © 1984 by Fernando Alegría and Stephen Kessler. Poems by permission of Latin American Literary Review Press.

PAULA GUNN ALLEN: "Elegy for My Son," and "Snowgoose," from *Coyote's Daylight Trip*, copyright © 1978 by Paula Gunn Allen. "He na Tye Woman," and "Mountain Song," from *Shadow Country*, copyright © 1982 by the Regents of the University of California, published by the American Indian Studies Center. Poems by permission of the author.

ALTA: "Veterans Day in Healdsburg," copyright © 1986 by Alta, by permission of the author.

ROBERT ANBIAN: "The Dying Man's Shame," "Oceanology," and "Old Woman," and from *Bohemian Airs & other Kefs*, copyright © 1982 by Robert Anbian, by permission of the author.

ROGER APLON: "If Your Skin," from *Stiletto*, copyright © 1976 by Roger Aplon. "Trailing the Army," from *By Dawn's Early Light at 120 Miles Per Hour*, copyright © 1983 by Roger Aplon. Reprinted by permission of Dryad Press.

JANICE BLUE: "St. Francis," from *In Good Old No-Man's Land*, copyright © 1978 by Janice Blue, by permission of the author.

KAREN BRODINE: "There Is A Refusal To Be Drowned," and "What She Did In My Dream," from *Slow Juggling*, copyright © 1975 by the Berkeley Poets' Workshop and Press, by permission of the publisher. "Girlfriends," from *Illegal Assembly*, copyright © 1980 by Karen Brodine, by permission of Hanging Loose Press. "the wolves were silver," from *Workweek*, copyright © 1977 by Kelsey St. Press, by permission of the publisher. "Censorship," appeared in *Sinister Wisdom # 24*, copyright © 1983 by Karen Brodine, by permission of the author.

JAMES BROUGHTON: "Nipples and cocks," from *Graffiti for the Johns of Heaven*, copyright © 1982 by James Broughton. "Shaman Psalm," from *Ecstasies*, copyright © 1983 by James Broughton. Poems reprinted by permission of Syzygy Press.

D.F. BROWN: "Illumination," and "Long Range Patrol," from *Returning Fire*, copyright © 1984 by D.F. Brown. "First Wish," "Poem—At first it's cold," and "Poem—I'm talking about boys," copyright © 1985 by D.F. Brown. Poems by permission of the author.

JANINE CANAN: "It's Her Birthday," "The Mother Cooks The Soup," and "A Woman, Head On Her Belly," from *Shapes of Self*, copyright © 1982 by Janine Canan, by permission of the author.

NEELI CHERKOVSKI: "Joshua," from *The Waters Reborn*, copyright © 1975 by Neeli Cherry, by permission of Red Hill Press. "There Is a Javelin," from *Clear Wind*, copyright © 1984 by Neeli Cherkovski, by permission of the author.

ELLEN COONEY: "rape," copyright © 1984 by Ellen Cooney, by permission of the author.

LUCHA CORPI: "Letter to Arturo," "Obsoletarium," and "Romance of the Little Girl," from *Palabras De Mediodia/Noon Words*, copyright © 1980 by Lucha Corpi and Catherine Rodriguez-Nieto, by permission of the author and the translator.

GREGORY CORSO: "The Whole Mess…Almost," from *Herald of the Autochtonic Spirit*, copyright © 1981 by Gregory Corso. Reprinted by permission of the New Directions Publishing Corporation.

CONTENTS

PRACTISING ANGELS

"When company falls silent, the French
say an angel is passing through."
—Edmund White

FRANCISCO X. ALARCÓN

PRAYER/ORACION

I want a god	quiero un dios
as my accomplice	de cómplice
who spends nights	que se trasnoche
in houses	en tugurios
of ill repute	de mala fama
& gets up late	y los sábados
on Saturday	se levante tarde
a god	un dios
whistling	que chifle
through the streets	por las calles
& trembling	y tiemble
before the lips	ante los labios
of his lover	de su amor
a god	un dios
waiting in line	que haga cola
at the entrance	a la entrada
of movie theaters	de los cines
& who likes to drink	y tome café
cafe au lait	con leche
a god	un dios
who spits	que escupa
blood from	sangre de
tuberculosis	tuberculoso
& doesn't even have	y no tenga ni
enough for bus fare	para el camión
a god	un dios
knocked down	que se desmaye
unconscious	de un macanazo
by the billy club	de policía
of a policeman	en un mitin
in a demonstration	de protesta
a god	un dios
pissing	que se orine
out of fear	de miedo ante

1

before the flaring	el resplandor
electrodes	de los electrodos
of torture	de tortura
a god	un dios
hurting	que le punce
to the last	hasta el último
bone	hueso
& biting the air	y muerda el aire
in pain	de dolor
a jobless god	un dios desempleado
a striking god	un dios en huelga
a hungry god	un dios hambriento
a fugitive god	un dios fugitivo
an exiled god	un dios en exilio
an enraged god	un dios encabronado
a god	un dios
longing	que anhele
from jail	desde la carcel
for a change	un cambio
in the order	en el orden
of things	de las cosas
I want a	quiero
more godlike	un dios
god	más dios

ROOTS

I carry
my roots
with me
all the time
rolled up
I use them
as my pillow

WOUNDED WORDS/PALABRAS HERIDAS

words
don't recognize me
if I come near them
wild like cats
they scratch
me

words
hurt me
like open wounds
no matter how much
I clean & treat them
never do they heal!

las
palabras
me desconocen
si me les acerco
hurañas como gatos
me rasguñan

a mí
me duelen
las palabras
como heridas abiertas
que por más que limpio y curo
nunca cicatrizan

FUGITIVE

I've had
to bear
the days
anonymously
like a shadow
slip
through the city
without raising
suspicions

I've avoided
innumerable
roads
jumped
every fence
fleeing

FRANCISCO X. ALARCÓN

always
with a haste
that bites
my heels
& barely
lets me breathe

hiding behind
so many
illusions
during
so many years
now
I don't
even recognize
the face of
my soul
nor remember
what brought me
to this fugitive's life

my crime
must have
been
as huge as
the darkness
found in
my punishment

above all
I've sought
the mute
company
of night

I've learned
to fake
almost everything
but
still
when next to you
I'm given away
by the empty
pounding
of my heart

DAVID MELTZER

THE RED SHOES

And I woke up dancing
    out of bed past kids crying in clusters
    mine hers anybody else's
    piled up writhing howling
    steamy cracked windows
    stink of ancient diapers sour milk
    cartoon rat whiskers crushed Raggedy
    broken Fisher-Price homes
    uncoiled rabbits Legos Tonka trucks
    Pacific mould on windowsills
    crowing black green alphabet dots
    burst to spread and mark monk-white
    walls crazed with Crayola faces
And I danced down the hallway lept over the dogs
    and cats hunting each other for food
    who turned to attack me like a *corps de ballet*
    but I was dancing and I'd never danced before
    music from all the radios propelled me
Into and out of rooms where my lives erased
    and I leapt into space free of sorrow or thought or art
And she pleaded with me to take her
But I said no it wouldn't work
I dance alone the radios are behind me
And she said will you leave me with the kids the rooms the TV
    brokendown kitchen nothing works
    muggers robbers raiders
    clawing at doors windows
    snipers vipers pirates
    oozing through old keyholes
    gurus prophets healers Jehovah's Witnesses
    fisting the frontdoor into a tissue
Yes yes I yelled dancing past her down the hall
Yes yes the radios behind me and before me
Music more conclusive than the sun
And I dance down Russian Hill into North Beach
    old nicotine ivory Italian gentlemen
    young Italian silk misogyny
    Beatnik survivors tubbed in jukebox coffins
    drunk on history and hippie hold-out

New Age hobos piss at the world passing by
  bent over double in doorway zoos
And I dance past Broadway's whores
  tattered bare butt blushing with belt welts
  ravaged vagina overlit hand-held camera
  porno filmhouse aisles I dance down
  break moviedreamer meditation
  breaking through tough screen
  leap a Nijinsky onto a rope
  sandbag through iron exit door into day
Dance into City Lights microcosm feudal culture
Everyone's a poet but I dance
Everyone's an editor but I dance
Everybody has a book nobody reads and I dance
  down an alley into Chinatown
  attacked by teenage Bruce Lee mafia
  karate and .38s
  but I leap higher than Confucius
  who didn't dance from his hut his palace
  his systems of etiquette
I dance to the city radio
  chien shanai cymbal dragon smash
  traffic cardiogram
  chopped off chickenheads
  trout scales scraped away
  crushed boiled crabshell crunch
  ladle day-old pork barbeque
  from stainless steel trays
  into takeout cardboard cartons
  white porcelain Kwan Yin cracks apart
  falls on marble Bank of Canton floor
  cameras on tourists like goiters
Everyone's amazed when I dance over dim-sum trays
  in black acrobat slippers
I need no food I'm fueled by dance
Radios are in front and back
  they're in my ears
  my mouth is a radio
  everything I see and hear is music
  everything I say
  everything is music I dance to
Dance to a mad speed-babbler's rap
  tapping like crazy
  Honey Coles hold your hat
  Fred watch out
  better believe it Bubbles
And no trace of sweat

And no thought and no art and true to each
    second my body moves over the fallen
    and the arising

    Gasping punk
    potsmoker
    rocked out
    bangs head
    ringing into
    iron lamp post

    Girl friend
    fried hair
    bleached tongue
    giggles black
    lipstick

                                        3:I:81

"EACH WORD THE WORD CREATING"

Each word the word creating
protecting life

all else like bayonets
goes against it

in death's ink sit soldiers
wrapping dead in book pages

the book weeps black blood
in their mouths

the book weeps white nerve flames
thread sewing dead eyes shut

the book weeping itself empty of words

the book a powder like ash of bones
warriors paint their faces to attack children

each word the word creating
protecting life in lights of song or silence
all else goes against it

LAMENTATION FOR JACK SPICER

Sir, I'm out of touch with stars.
The bar's closed. We go
stumbling down Grant to Columbus
to the Park to somebody's parked car.
Somebody says, Let's all go to Ebbe's.
Says Ebbe, Sure, why not, let's all go.
We're gone in the car, piled in the back
seat, breathing wine on the windowpanes.
This, seven years ago. Tonight

It is pain to realize you're dead,
your last book on the shelf,
your last words to a nation
not indivisible but invisible;
a nation that will never will its mystery to poets
who even in Greece werent poet enough to handle man
nor touch the dark forms. Gone.
Maybe that night it was Marco
who fell back upon a park bush.

We left him there to sleep.

JANICE MIRIKITANI

ASSAULTS AND INVASIONS

Linette was beaten daily.
He said she wasn't any good, dumb and weak even for
a woman.

Every time I'd see her, face swollen like a bruised soft
peach, lip hanging big and purple over her chin, her eyes
bled hunger and helplessness. When he would start in on
her, she could only defend with fingernails and sweat and
a tongue fat with broken veins and angry words. She is
105 pounds powerless to his 200 pound body, and she
opens her legs like murdered wheat. She moved out
several times, this time reporting him to the police,
begged the courts to restrain him. He found her, and
when she wouldn't whimper or cry or open her thighs,
this time, he with his razor began to slice small slivers of
flesh from her breasts, her crotch, her belly, like scaling
a fish, until her body bubbled like a red carp. Her mouth
so thick with pain, she could hardly scream stop it. stop
it. stop it.

Today, United States Marines invade Grenada. Why
do I think of this woman's life? Like sirens that hurt the
ears of dogs, like insidious water dripping through rusty
drains, like the pain of flesh slowly slivered and peeled,
we want to scream, stop it.

Yesterday, Benigno Aquino, bringing hope home like
a day full of poppies, died. Undisguised murder in the
open air, his blood darkening into tunnels of the earth.
Marcos' assassins pick their teeth, and the day spills the
stench of rotten fish. We beat our fists against the
windows, weeping in the passageways...stop it.

Linette barely lived. The police did nothing. The
courts shrugged their shoulders and yawned. When she
went home from the hospital, he was waiting, enraged
by her acts of defiance. He took his razor and burning
cigaret and made her hurt, made her bleed. She knew this
time he would show he could control her death. She

9

wanted to survive. The bullet went through his heart,
and she thought she saw for the first time in his eyes,
surprise that she had made him stop it.

So why do I think of this woman on the day of the
invasion in Grenada?

We cannot catch our breath, our tongues too thick
with rage, beating our fists against windows. Each day
people disappear in Chile, Paraguay, Honduras, Uruguay,
Guatemala. Assaults against the sovereignty of Nicaragua.
Blockades against Cuba, genocide in El Salvador, murders
in Manila, apartheid in South Africa.

Each day the ism's like a boot attempt to crush us:
racism, capitalism, imperialism, materialism, sexism,
colonialism, ageism, classism, militarism.

> We must breathe deeply.
> Escape through the windows.
> We must gather, find each other.
> Hear the heartbeats, the power in our veins.
> We must clear our voices,
> take action to make ourselves known.
> We must stop it
> stop it.
> stop it.

—excerpt from fictional prose

A SONG FOR YOU

for Cecil

You laugh
your big laugh
your hands
    like wings
    or a dancer's wish
enclosures for the last/first sleep

I want to
hold
suck
taste your skin
breathing in
that dark, deep

I want to
bathe your limbs
like trees
your roots
entangled hard in mine

and walk your back
from Tokyo
to Dar Es Salaam
lulling you with genmai tea

touch me
sing me
make me born
together we will
sound lost bones
and color their flesh

yes,
we will hold
the sea
you and i
and bring
the deep/moist/soft
mouth
to the shores
of all
our continents.

JUNGLE ROT AND OPEN ARMS

for a Vietnam Veteran brother, ex-prisoner

Leavenworth
and jungle rot

brought him
back to us
brimming with hate
and disbelief
in love or
sympathy.

his johnnywalker red
eyes
tore at my words
shred my flesh
made naked my
emptiness.

my anger
for the enemy heads
of state
boiled to nothing
          nothing
in the wake
of his rage

Jungle rot
had sucked his bones,
his skin fell
like the monsoon,
his brain
in a cast in Leavenworth.

In the midst
of genocide
he fell in love
in Vietnam.

               "Her hair was
                long and dark — like yours"
                        he said
               "her eyes held the
                sixth moon
                and when she smiled
                the sky opened
                and I fell through.

                I would crawl
                in the tall grasses
                to her village

and sleep the war
away with her
like a child on my thighs

I did not know
of the raid

and woke

with her arm
still clasping mine

I could not find
the rest of her

so I buried her arm
and marked my grave."

We sat in a silence
that mocks fools
that lifts us to the final language.

his breath sapped by B-52's
his eyes blinded by the blood of children
his hands bound to bayonets
his soul buried in a shallow grave

i stood amidst
his wreckage
and wept for myself.

so where is my
political education? my
rhetoric that answers to everything? my
theory into practice? my
intensification of life in art?

words
are
like
the stone,
the gravemarker
over an arm
in Vietnam.

D.F. BROWN

FIRST WISH

I don't remember Viet Nam.
I want to keep sleeping my dream.
I want to turn my head around.
I want to look the other way.
I want to dance in the obvious,
counting second chances.

LONG RANGE PATROL

Tense
again there as a
cat and sure   I
can see in the dark
this blanket bulletproof
the attack will come
on the other side
they won't
get me they don't   I am
home   it is
daylight
         then
our sentry blows
his claymore   we
all let go and I wish
I had dug deeper or it
wasn't me or
my friends hold me
I am home   it is
daylight

POEM

At first it's cold
A wish for long underwear
Then something pulled close up

All night in a blur, a fire
And you say you understand
Enough black coffee to choke morning

A lot of words strung up to move your heart
The childish fear where things come true
The year you needed more baseball

Days you squeeze out near the finish
Something in the holy somehow
In the DO DAH distance, bases loaded

A chopper to third
The sacrifice for lawn gods

ILLUMINATION

no sunrise here   three layers of green
give a day a lime glow   evening lasts five
grey minutes   the dark stays all night
lighting a smoke marks the spot for anybody
everything is a dead giveaway

        the new L T dreams up some movement
he has to see   he is truly possessed
has been crying for his girl   she is all
he needs but a little light in the jungle
will make it   go away   he radios base
crank up the 105's   fire illumination

        a we-know-they-know-where-we-are-at
I hope we don't find them   I've been there
seen the pictures

POEM

I'm talking about boys
who die for nothing,

or at best
for some god damned hill

the command abandons
the next day.

I'm talking blood
you suckers.

I'm talking
19 from Alabama.

Some kid
who just lost his guts

and no bandage is big enough.
I'm talking blood.

KIRBY DOYLE

RAGA / FOR DAVID

David, you are so beautiful today
and I have not seen you for a week!

O my meal today,
you should have seen!

I had tubers, finely roasted,
yams they were, there were two —

and sweet-butter melted in,
and shavings from my onion,

Salt and pepper!
O a fine meal.

And after, I had ragas,
and coffee, very thick
to please with my smoking
and I thought very still
my thinking, 'God is served God
as the only fit food.'

My meal today, O
David, you should have seen!

"I HAVE TWO HEARTS"

I have two hearts
upon my breast —
call one the sun and one the moon —
by one all golden eyed I come,
by the other a silver fool.

ZAHIR

The lily has barely
  escaped the cruelty
  of my tire,

but ah the rose,
the rose bids aim
  my wanton arrow
higher.

"I CAME TO THE TOP OF THIS MOUNTAIN"

I came to the top of this
mountain with only an ax,
some rice, and my son...
at last no books have followed
me...
If these flys were poems
I could die now
a happy man...

                August 21, 1966

JAMES BROUGHTON

SHAMAN PSALM

Listen Brothers Listen
The alarms are on fire
The oracles are strangled
Hear the pious vultures
condemning your existence
Hear the greedy warheads
calling for your death
Quick while there's time
Take heed Take heart
Claim your innocence
Proclaim your fellowship
Reach to each other
Connect one another
and hold

Rescue your lifeline
Defy the destroyers
Defy the fat vandals
They call for a nation
of castrated bigots
They promise a reward
of disaster and shame
Defy them Deny them
Quick while there's hope
Renovate man
Insist on your brotherhood
Insist on humanity
Love one another
and live

Release your mind from
the handcuffs of guilt
Take off your blinders
Focus your insight
Take off the bandages
that infect your fears
See your wounds heal when
you know your birthright
Men are not foes
Men are born loving

welcome being tingled by
the touch of devotion
Honor one another
or lose

Come Brothers Waken
Uproot hostility
Root out the hypocrites
Warm up your phoenix
to arouse a new era
Disarm the cutthroats
Sever the loggerheads
Offset the history
of torment and curse
Man is the species
endangered by man
Quick while there's time
Abandon your rivalries
or mourn

Deflate pugnacity
Magnify friendliness
Off with your mask
Off with your face
Dump the false guides
who travel the warpaths
Uncover your loving
Discover surrender
Rise in your essence to
the tender occasion
Unwrap your radiance
and brighten your crew
Value one another
or fall

Come forth unabashed
Come out unbuttoned
Bury belligerence
Resurrect frolic
Only through body can
you clasp the divine
Only through body can
you dance with the god
In every man's hand
the gift of compassion
In every man's hand
the beloved connection

Trust one another
or drown

Banish animosity
Summon endearment
You are kindred to
each one you greet
each one you deal with
crossing the world
Salute the love ability
in all those you meet
Elicit the beauty that
hides in all flesh
Let freedom of feeling
liberate mankind
Love one another
at last

Hold nothing back
Hold nothing in
Romp and commingle
out in the open
Parade your peculiar
Shine your monkey
Rout the sourpuss
Outrage the prig
Quick while there's room
revel in foolhardy
Keep fancies tickled
Grow fond of caress
Go forthright together
or fail

Affirm your affection
Be laughing in wisdom
You are a miracle
dismissed as a moron
You are a godbody
avoiding holiness
Claim your dimension
Insist on redemption
Love between men will
anachronize war
bring joy into office
and erogenate peace
Accept one another
and win

Relish new comrades
Freshen new dreams
Speak from the heart
Sing from the phallus
Keep holy bounce in
your intimate ballgames
Sexual fervor can
leap over galaxy
outburst the sun
football the moon
Give way to love
Give love its way
Ripen one another
or rot

Extend your vision
Stretch your exuberance
Offer your body to
the risks of delight
where soul can run naked
spirit jump high
Taste the divine on
the lips of lover
Savor the divine on
the thigh of friend
Treasure the divinity
that ignites the orgasm
Surprise the eagles
and soar

Let the weapons rust
Let the powers crumble
Open your fists
into embraces
Open your armslength
into loving circles
Be champions of hug
Be warriors of kiss
Prove in beatitude
a new breed of man
Prove that comradeship
is the crown of the gods
Cherish one another
and thrive

Listen Brothers Listen
The alarms are too late
This is the hour for

amorous revolt
Dare to take hold
Dare to take over
Be heroes of harmony
in bedfellow bliss
Man must love man
or war is forever
Outnumber the hawks
Outdistance the angels
Love one another
or die

"NIPPLES AND COCKS"

Nipples and cocks
nipples and cocks
Nothing tickles the palate like
nipples and cocks

Lose your appetite for
clippers and clocks
by trying a tipple of
nipples and cocks

Up with your T shirts
Down with your jocks
Tempt your tastebuds with
nipples and cocks

Don't riddle your brow
or rot in your box
It's nicer to nibble on
nipples and cocks

No need to be fancy
or unorthodox
Just try a plain diet of
nipples and cocks

Nipples and cocks
nipples and cocks
Nothing tickles the palate like
nipples and cocks

JANINE CANAN

IT'S HER BIRTHDAY

It's her birthday. She almost forgets how many years—more than the leaves on her orchids, more than the cups in her cupboard, more than the stones she's gathered along the shore. Her age is like a large bouquet with the white daisies and thorny berries of her childhood, the irises yellow and purple of her youth, the roses of her middle age. She is like a rose although she doesn't think so. Rose of an extremely unusual shade: lower petals long and darkly curling under, upper petals wet still, and closed like the tiny fingers of a newborn, bright starched petals standing out at the sides, finely balanced one over the other. She hangs there, wonderfully, in the early evening shadow. As someone bends over to smell her deeply private fragrance.

A WOMAN, HEAD ON HER BELLY

A woman, head on her belly, the moon, the long curve of the shore, waves lapping and green, a woman, head on her belly, the moon, the long curve of the shore glowing, woman, a head on her belly, the moon, the long curve of the shore glowing, thin hips of the palm tree, waves lapping and green, floating over her, this form that silences all others, a woman, head on her belly, the moon, the long curve of the shore glowing, the thin arc of the palm tree, her body deep, soft as a wave, lapping and green, rising to breast, sinking to waist, then lifting over her hip into the wet sand of her thigh, curves that carry her every which way, hand, cheek, lips, a woman, my head on her belly, the moon, the long curve of the shore, waves lapping and green, the long slim hip of the palm tree, hand stunned by the softness, rises to breast, falling to waist and over her hip, slippery, this smooth stone that never will never speak, the long green curve of the shore lapping, the thin curve of the palmtree, up to her breast, into her waist, down and over...

THE MOTHER COOKS THE SOUP

The mother cooks the soup. The mother stands over the open fire, sun pouring down onto the straw roof, stirring the soup. When the soup is ready and the sun has set, the family is seated in a circle in the hut. The soup is placed in the center. The father picks up the bowl and turns it, sucking up the rich piece of meat, then passes the bowl to the eldest son, who takes a deep gulp and passes it on to his brother, who drinks and passes it on. So from hand to hand it reaches the youngest, who sips out the dregs and returns the bowl empty to the mother. She sniffs and carefully licks its fine slick sides, then carries it back to the kitchen.

DIANE DI PRIMA

LOBA IN CHILDBED

She lay in bed, screaming, the boat
carried her to the heart of the mandala
sweat stuck
hair to her forehead, she
lay back, panting, remembering
it was what she *should* do. Skull boat
carried her to the heart of her womb, red
pulsing eye of her spirit. She saw
soul shine shoaled on rocks, flint edges
of rocky pelvic cage, caught, swirls
of bland liquid eddying round
curls of bright
red-gold hair, she
screamed, for him, for herself, she
tried to open, to widen tunnel, the rock
inside her tried to crack, to chip away
bright spirit hammered at it w / his
soft foamy head
              she cried out
bursting from the heart
                  of the devastated
mandala, skull boat grew wings
                      she fluttered
thru amniotic seas to draw him on.

        Gold
        swirling sun, gold
        swirling folds of
        kesa, enfolding, blinding
        her opaquer eyes

        the speck
        of red alchemic gold
        caught in black
        womb spasm
        struggled weaker
        toward earthlight
        she offered.

It was
round stone head monolith
lying in Colombian jungle
tried to articulate, to burst
out of her.

It was
line drawing bird soul
as in hieroglyphs or in
Indian drawing fluttered
down to meet her

Snatches of brief music, unremitting
white pain, his only
signals

Dark cave. Dark forces countering
magic w / magic. No time
to navigate now; no white
quartz, no lapis, incense, blessed
flowery water. Only
shrill mantra scream, arch
mudra of tossing pain
torture of watching spirit, measured
in pulse beat   from wires tied
to heart of her cunt, center
of her womb. Have the oceanic
presences deserted her?

                She walked moaning
                into dry heart of
                sandstone continent
                snatched pale
                phosphorescing son
                from red cliffs,
                the sun
                flashed like pain
                behind her eyes

Was he limp, did he stir
w / life, did she hear
his soft breath in her ear?

THE LOBA SINGS TO HER CUB

O my mole, sudden & perfect
golden gopher tunneling
to light, o separate(d)
strands of our breath!
               Bright silver
threads of spirit
          O quicksilver
spurt of fist, scansion of
unfocussed eyeball,
             grace of yr
cry, or song, my
cry or
     you lie warm,   wet on the
soggy pelt of my
       hollowed
belly, my
       bones curve up
to embrace you.

REVOLUTIONARY LETTER #32

not western civilization, but civilization itself
is the disease which is eating us
not the last five thousand years, but the last twenty thousand
are the cancer
not modern cities, but the city, not
capitalism, but ism, art, religion, once they are
separate enough to be seen and named, named art named
religion, once they are not
simply the daily acts of life which bring the rain, bring bread,
                           heal, bring
the herds close enough to hunt, birth the children
simply the acts of song, the acts of power, now lost
to us these many years, not killing a few white men will bring
back power, not killing all the white men, but killing
the white man in each of us, killing the desire
for brocade, for gold, for champagne brandy, which sends
people out of the sun and out of their lives to create

COMMODITY for our pleasure, what claim
do we have, can we make, on another's time, another's
life blood, show me
a city which does not consume the air and water
for miles around it, mohenjo-daro was a blot
on the village culture of India, the cities of Egypt sucked
the life of millions, show me
an artifact of city which has the power
as flesh has power, as spirit of man
has power

REVOLUTIONARY LETTER #20

(for Huey Newton)

I will not rest
till men walk free & fearless on the earth
each doing in the manner of his blood
& tribe, peaceful in the free air

till all can seek, unhindered
the shape of their thought
no black cloud fear or guilt
between them & the sun, no babies burning
young men locked away, no paper world
to come between flesh & flesh in human
encounter

till the young women
come into their own, honored & fearless
birthing strong babes
loving & dancing

till the young men can at last
lose some of their sternness, return
to young men's thoughts, till laughter
bounces off our hills and fills
our plains

KUSH/HIBAKUSHA

Enola Gay

WIDE ISLAND (Bird over Mountain)

HIROSHIMA

See the open hand of land

When will the States
Show Compassion

B-29

Zero Yolk Bright Brighter BRIGHTEST Whiter Blue White Fireball
Fire curves down curves in curves up curves out
whorl whorling whorl Burning wave white Burning wave gray
dust rising blaze gray dust rising flame curl flame
curl flame flash blank iron roaring blank indrawing blank
stone rippling blank melting blank girders twisting fold in
walls into winds flash men into shadows cut granite
disintegrating sidewalk woman walking out of existence
                    Thundering Walls
Burning Wind Vaporizing bone flesh gone with metal gust
Shock Structure Dissolves Swirling Rubble torn structure giving way
claw of flame bench girl claw of flame dust
Breaking Branches Breaking Power Lines Snake in the Wind
blank indrawing blank Shock Wave window bursting piece pieces
concussion concussion buckle shatter blown out dark dust rising

Being Thrown   You are buried in where you are
Building Skeleton gray dust hung Building Toppling Burning Buddha
Burning gates Building collapse gray dust rising crack crash
gray dust falling Building aflame black column spiralling smoke
Black billowing smoke spiral black column smoke bellowing flame
House caves in   lines fall   dead youth   burnt horse
Breaking Beams   a man bends over a mangled child
Window Flames   Man holding his head   Kneels down   Sighs
Burning Bank   water body face down water water bank
Smoking Tree   smoldering child grasses burning water warm shade
Bleeding Middle of Rice Paddy   Broken Well of Now
Burning Road   final breaths   Moon Moving   Boat of Wounds
Burning grasses dead child of the bird smoking grasses
A Woman Looking For Her Boy   MOUND OF RUBBLE
man crawling rubble tangled twisted burnt rubble smoking tree
rubble fire dead twisted dead tangled rubble singed broken
wrenched twisted rubble bicycle rubble blaze Exploding Shock
brickwall burning grasses water water man following man splashing
water water water burning grasses broken wreckage flaming car
smashed dead bent twisted wind swirling twisted dead tangled
burning rubble Structure Falling girl running scream skin burns
rubble dead smoking rubble radiator street Mother child hurrying
tangled fire burnt telephone pole lines sagging twisted tangled
Smoke rising Structure Broken bent split burnt cracked torn
flattened pushed in knocked down fractured stump shaken crushed
pulled away tangled wreck burning fragment shredded shambles dust
torn out shattered burst burnt thrown down smoke rising
white gray black white gray black gray black gray
black black white black gray black white black black
gray gray gray black gray gray black black gray
black gray black gray black gray black gray white

When the sun came into our hands
Existence was burnt

WILLIAM MAHER

STREETCORNERS OF THE WORLD UNITE!

who have i not seen standing there
i have hesitated on streetcorners all over the world
streetcorners
where i discovered idleness
(IT MADE A BEGGAR OF MY TIME)
streetcorners
where i staged loneliness not to be afraid
streetcorners
where i made a tragic spectacle of myself
streetcorners
where i pretended to wait for a bus
so as not to look like a man with no future
i took my first caress there alone
STREETCORNERS OF THE WORLD UNITE!
who have i not seen standing there
idle men make good kings
observe that idiot savant
(SHE PEES DEFIANTLY IN HER PANTS)
that's my girl
(HOW WELL I REMEMBER YOUR FIERCE BLUE DEFIANT EYES)
you stand forever at the four corners of my heart
who have i not seen standing there
it's the greatest show on earth
when you have no prophecies left in your guts
when there is no love interest to feed
no great cause to espouse
no money to throw away
no deadlines on the boards
no religion's got its cross or sword in you
no rendezvous with destiny to keep
who have i not seen standing there
STREETCORNERS OF THE WORLD UNITE!
back up against the wall?
you're not standing in anyone's way
i myself have not taken an order for six months
it does something to the character of a face
(HOW DO YOU WANT YOUR TIME, CHUMP?
  IT SERVED TO YOU, OR YOU SERVED TO IT?)
show me a person who never took an order in their life

i'll show you a happy man
(A SIGHT FEW PEOPLE HAVE SEEN)
how many of you are afraid of them?
don't want to be seen standing around doing nothing
it wouldn't look good on your resume
you might run into someone you know
(HAVE TO EXPLAIN YOURSELF)
it wouldn't look good to look like somebody
with nothing but time on their hands
STREETCORNERS OF THE WORLD UNITE!
who have i not seen standing there
i watched my first sunrise and moon go down from one
i watched the first woman i loved turn away from me
i waited till i thought i would die
(SHE NEVER CAME BACK)
who have i not seen standing there
hoping to be recognized by the crowd
hoping someone remembered they'd forgotten something
(THEY'D FORGOTTEN AT THE LAST MINUTE TO SAY)
hoping they had the hour wrong, the place, the day
streetcorners
where passersby took me for dead
where dogs mistook me for the tires of a car
(A CASE OF MISTAKEN IDENTITY)
streetcorners
where i clung to fire hydrants for my life
(AFRAID I WOULD GO UP IN FLAMES IF I MOVED)
streetcorners
where police questioned my motives for standing there
(I AM WAITING FOR A DAY WHEN THE LIGHTS WON'T
  CHANGE, OFFICER)
streetcorners
i wrote my first lines from one
(I'LL PROBABLY WRITE MY LAST)
streetcorners
where you always have at least two choices
(STAY WHERE YOU ARE, OR LEAVE)
ask Hamlet where he'd be without one
STREETCORNERS OF THE WORLD UNITE!
who have i not seen standing there
the nights are lonely with them
the meeting place of murderers and their victims
drug addicts and their connections
hero worshipers and their look-a-likes
religious fanatics and bird watchers
uniformed officers and plain-clothes men
prostitutes and their potential suicides

revolutionaries and hypochondriacs
do-gooders and good for nothings
who have i not seen standing there
streetcorners
where i met Jean d'Arc on many a late afternoon
streetcorners
where i practiced my opening lines
(FOR A MEETING THAT NEVER TOOK PLACE)
streetcorners
open twenty four hours, that know
our bag ladies are falling stars in the night
(WHO IMAGINE THEY PLEASE THE MOON
  BY SLEEPING BENEATH ITS GLOW)
streetcorners
i have always loved you
(THOUGH SOME NIGHTS I USED YOU LIKE A WHORE)
streetcorners
where the poems are scribbled on napkins
(THAT WILL SAVE THIS COUNTRY)
STREETCORNERS OF THE WORLD UNITE!
who have i not seen standing there
a poet locked out of his hotel till he borrows the rent
a dying old woman's last address on this earth
streetcorners
are rivers, my friends
the nights are lonely with them
streetcorners
THE LAST LIGHTED PLACE IN AMERICA
a single lightbulb overhead
a creation of Edison
(WE INHERIT HIS LONELINESS THROUGH THE NIGHT)
STREET CORNERS OF THE WORLD UNITE!
you're all that's left to us now
AND WE'RE A LONG WAY FROM HOME!

JANICE BLUE

SAINT FRANCIS

Now I don't know much
about Catholics and I don't like
Romans no way, but I tell you

this little bit about Francis, saint
of this city and that talked to the birds...

Francis he have his native birds and then
Francis he have his migrant birds, but
all the birds flock to Francis...Francis say

What is the news bird? and the bird might say,
Not so good Francis, last week urban renewal
                    plowed down 13 streets of old
                    Beale St., Memphis from the river...

        Francis say that's too bad bird,
        but come on in until it's over...
        Yea, come on in until it's over.

        Whatever the Telegraph Hill Association
        says, that's what kind of dude Francis
        is. that's what kind of dude francis
        is...who wouldn't pay a buck
        toll to get into this place?

                              —North Beach '77

THOM GUNN

SWEET THINGS

He licks the last chocolate ice cream
from the scabbed corners of his mouth.
Sitting in the sun on a step
outside the laundromat,
mongoloid Don turns his crewcut head
and spies me coming down the street.
'Hi!' He says it with the mannered
enthusiasm of a fraternity brother.
'Take me cross the street!?' part
question part command. I hold
the sticky bunch of small fingers in mine
and we stumble across. They sell
peaches and pears over there,
the juice will dribble down your chin.
He turns before I leave him,
saying abruptly with the same
mixture of order and request
'Gimme a quarter!?' I
don't give it, never have, not to him,
I wonder why not, and as I
walk on alone I realize
it's because his seven-year-old mind
never recognizes me, me
for myself, he only says hi
for what he can get, quarters to
buy sweet things, one after another,
he goes from store to store, from
candy store to ice cream store to
bakery to produce market, unending
quest for the palate's pleasure. Then
out to panhandle again,
more quarters, more sweet things.

My errands are toothpaste,
vitamin pills and a book of stamps.
No self-indulgence there.
But who's this coming up? It's
John, no Chuck, how
could his name have slipped my mind.

Chuck gives a one-sided smile, he stands
as if fresh from a laundromat,
a scrubbed cowboy, Tom Sawyer
grown up, yet stylish, perhaps
even careful, his dark hair
slicked back in the latest manner.
When he shakes my hand I feel
a dry finger playfully bending inward
and touching my palm in secret.
'It's a long time
since we got together,' says John.
Chuck, that is. The warm teasing
tickle in the cave of our handshake
took my mind off toothpaste,
snatched it off, indeed.
How handsome he is in
his lust and energy, in his
fine display of impulse.
Boldly 'How about now?' I say
knowing the answer. My boy
I could eat you whole. In the long pause
I gaze at him up and down and
from his blue sneakers back to the redawning
one-sided smile. We know our charm.
We know delay makes pleasure great.
In our eyes, on our tongues,
we savour the approaching delight
of things we know yet are fresh always.
Sweet things. Sweet things.

LAWRENCE FERLINGHETTI

THE LOVE NUT

I go into the men's room Springfield bus station
on the way back to Muhlenberg County
and see this nut in the mirror
Who let in this weirdo Who let in this creep?
He's the kind writes I LOVE YOU on toilet walls and wants to
    embrace everybody in the lobby He writes his phone number
    inside a heart on the wall He's some kinda pervert Mister
    Eros the Great Lover
He wants to run up to everybody in the waiting room and kiss
    them on the spot and say Why aren't we friends and lovers
    Can I go home with you You got anything to drink or smoke
    Let's you and me get together The time is now or sooner
He wants to take all the stray dogs and cats and people home
    with him and turn them on to making love all the time
    wherever
He wants to scatter poems from airplanes across the landscape
    He's some kinda poetic nut Like he thinks he's Dylan
    Thomas and Bob Dylan rolled together with Charlie Chap-
    lin thrown in
He wants to lip-read everybody's thoughts and feelings and
    longings He's a dangerous nut He's gotta be insane He has
    no sense of sin
He wants to heat up all the dead-looking people the unhappy-
    looking people in bus stations and airports He wants to heat
    up their beds He wants to open their bodies and heads
He's some kinda airhead rolling stone He don't wanna be alone
    He may be queer on men
He's the kind addresses everybody on buses making them laugh
    and look away and then look back again
He wants to get everyone to burst out laughing and sighing and
    crying and singing and dancing and kissing each other in-
    cluding old ladies and policemen
He's gotta be mad he's so glad to be alive He's real strange He's
    got the hots for humanity one at a time He wants to kiss
    your breasts He wants to lie still between them singing in a
    low voice
He wants everyone to lie down together and roll around together
    moaning and singing and having visions and orgasms He
    wants to come in you He wants you to come with him He

wants us all to come together One hot world One heartbeat
He wants he wants us all to lie down together in Paradise in the
Garden of Love in the Garden of Delights and couple
together like a train a chain-reaction a chain-letter-of-love
around the world on hot nights
He wants he wants he wants! He's gotta be crazy Call the cops
Take him away!

THE REBELS

Star-stricken still
            we lie under them
                        in dome of night
      as they wheel about
                  in their revolutions
      forming and reforming
                              (oh not for us!)
                  their splendiferous
                        phosphor fabrications

Ah the wheelwright of it
                        (whoever he or she or it)
            chief fabricator
                        of the night of it
            of the night to set it in
                              this cut-glass
                                    diamond diagram

Upstairs
      in the lighted attic
            under the burning eaves
                              of time
      lamps hung out
            (to guide far more far-out voyagers
                  than ourselves)

Still antic stars
            shoot out
                        burst out—
                              errant rebels

                    even there
        in the perfect pattern
                        of some utopia
            shooting up
                        tearing the
                            silver web
            of perfect symmetry

As in a palm of hand
            the perfect plan of line
                    of life and heart and head
        struck across a sudden
                        by one
                            cataclysmic tear

Yet all not asunder
                all not lost to darkness
        all held together still
                    at some still center
            even now
        in the almost incendiary dawn
    as still another
                rebel burning bright
                strikes its match upon
                            our night

HE WITH THE BEATING WINGS

The lark has no tree
        the crow no roost
    the owl no setting place
        the nightingale
            no certain song
And he with the beating wings
        no place to light
           in the neon dawn
     his tongue too long ago
        retuned
   by those ornithologists
        the state has hired
    to make sure
      the bird population of the world
    remains stable
       and pinioned
There is no need
    to clip its claws
Its tongue will do
    Tether the tongue
 and all falls fallow
   The wild seed drops
     into nothingness
Tether the tongue
   and all falls
     into silence
 a condition ever desired
     by tyrants
   not least of which is
      the great state
  with its benevolent birdwatchers
    with their nets and binoculars
watching out for
   the wild one
He that bears Eros
    like a fainting body
He that bears
    the gold bough
  He
   with the beating wings

KATHLEEN FRASER

CARELESS OF ALL HIS ADVICE, FLOWERS.

With the ability of some, the flowers, the sight of him bending the
night's two lakes, that untrained relation of craving to thought. She
dreams of him as a woman whose dark hair has been recently bleached.
A sympathetic Harlow blonde. White satin without seams. She seems to
row in one lake and sail on the other. At night, the splash does not travel
far. The others stay up endlessly—eating and drinking (things unutter-
ably sweet).

"THE CERTAINTY OF BYZANTINE TENDENCIES",
SHE READS.

This sweet curl and cold cove of Acanthus, oh leaf-bearing thought in
stone, when we consider what has stood! (Strokes the feather in her
pocket.) Gift of thumb, its opposites; time inside a person, worn
threads of your cape dazzle us, oh lover of birds we didn't notice! Our
muscles ache from the simple climb. These stones the length of tubs,
with their tiny ridges, catch us. Behind shutters the dark. Eyes of she
who cuts and washes. Cuts and washes.

WISHING MY TYPEWRITER WERE A PIANO

Keys, if you were attached to catgut, a vibration of animal whose
cry
is a keening...

but you are single windows,
showing O to suggest the sound I cannot make,
striking D for the man who hides and seeks in the small places
of my mouth,
clearing to K which is myself who has been pure light,
now curling against the changing weather, throat raw with
expectation.

You lack the mystery of unknown scales, are precise with each
stab
of my fingers, commit me to the blush of my own yearning.

Are you giving me your real thoughts? How can I know?

(He told me of looking at the woman he was to marry, of
understanding his hate
for her, of smiling...was it that smile tucked into my drawer this
morning?)

If you were a piano and my hands tuned,
keys, I would play the clear notes of black and white
and Mendelssohn would listen. The notes would sing of my
doubt.

MERLE WOO

UNTITLED

In the deepest night and a full moon,
at once riding the flying mare and being her
my own pumping broad wings, ascending higher—

My legs around that great horse's neck
not riding
but my body singing down under
in front of the beautiful dark head
feeling her moist tongue in my center—

I am risking my life for these moments,
My head possibly dashed against the rocks.

Now riding with our rhythms matching,
the exertion of her back's muscles and
the mounting pulsations between my thighs—

Higher and soaring through mist and above mountains
shaped like jagged spires
the cold thin air ripping through my lungs—

We finish.
And you lay your head on my thigh,
your wings enfolding my legs, and we rest.

Fall 1981

HOWARD HART

AFTER A FRENCH POEM OF JACQUES PREVERT

it's terrible
the tiny noise of a hardboiled egg cracked on a counter
   terrible
  when it's fixed in the head of a hungry man
 the hungry man is terrible too
his hungry face
        when
        when he looks at himself at six in the morning
        in a department store window
        face the color of dust
      and he can hardly see himself
       says to hell with what he looks like
       screw it
dreams
something the size of his dust-colored face
       that it's a steak
               juicy
      or even anything big and tasty

his jaws start working
slow
he grinds his teeth
      slowly
because this world has his head on a platter
and there's nothing he can do about it
    but count 1 2 3 on his fingers
1 2 3
now it's 3 days since he ate last
it can't go on
    it goes on tho
    3 days
    3 nights
    without eating
   and in all these windows
        meats bottles pastry
     motionless sea food in cans
      cans behind windows
      windows behind cops
cops behind fears

all that protection for six lousy sardines

and further on in another place
big cups of coffee   danish
          he don't walk straight
        and inside the head
        a swarm of words
        a swarm
sardines
hardboiled eggs   coffee in big cups
coffee with a shot of rum
coffee plenty light
coffee cream
cream coffee
coffee crime
          rum

        a man well thought of in his neighborhood
        was throttled in plain daylight
the killer the culprit took off him
eighty cents,
        that's 2 big cups of coffee
        —twenty cents
        2 danish and butter
        and a fifteen cent tip

it's terrible
the tiny noise of a hardboiled egg
cracked on a counter
terrible
when fixed in the head of a hungry man.

"WHEN THE GODS SMELLED THE HUMANS COMING ON EARTH"

When the Gods smelled the humans coming on earth,
they decided to split for awhile. They packed
their things, went off in their fine white chariots.
But like most people who move fast: they forgot
one thing...the wine, they left the wine to us.

LA RUCHE

Chagall
    I can't find Apollinaire's poem
So I'll write one of my own

Now an upturned house is not cursed
If it is upturned that The Lord may enter

And a cow that flies
    is a cow with true milk for children

I learned about you from Raïssa Maritain
Her little book held your agony between two jewels
    an amethyst and a topaz
And that's where I learned about Apollinaire too

It was an Ohio Sunday morning
    blue and dull
    with beautiful trees all over
    I was growing up
And only remembered that you had stuck by me
    once when looking at your painting in a museum
    I ogled and three chic people laughed at me
I have always played one of your violins
    and walked over houses

The reason that I am writing now
    probably
Is a week ago
    reading my poems
I started praying for Raïssa Maritain
And the people caught on
               prayed too
Although they didn't know it

Cendrars Chagall
We only love people when they are dead
And we can't embarrass ourselves
    by more personal contact
Chagall
    I say this while you are alive
Send me one of the clouds over your little
            town of Vence

And I will turn it into an orange subway car
Commemorating you now and forever
      in New York City
Where your cows musicians and lovers
Would hurt themselves on the buildings
      flying around as they do
      in your painting

GREEN DRUM SOLO

Your eyes are two black beads on a silver table
I call to you out of magnolias
Breast to breast to breast
Could they be speaking to one another?
Could they? On a pond in Holland
I know only too well
Tall swan to tall swan
They kiss below the full moon
      jars of honey that creep across a pantry
I find your hips inside my thighs
Really?
When placing my hand there I can almost feel your bones
      sometimes
The boats flow backwards into the water...Certainly?
I find myself within the whimper of dogs and within cars
      being repaired on Thursday afternoon
Also the "whaps" that concierges make as they clean a floor...
Her death shall be the blending of apple and emerald

Fingers which extend
Certainly...you have never seen it
The nape of your neck has a black pearl
The legs before my face can only be ivory

ELLEN COONEY

RAPE

the last night of school glad to be
free of the male students
still begging to follow the women home
took a bus to old friends and watched
"Wild Strawberries" on tv then
left when everyone went to bed
Tenth Avenue was still as I walked
to get the bus long past midnight
and I waited
and waited and California Street
was still and no bus came
and home was three miles away
a car pulled up and a man got out
friendly I thought asked if I knew
where he could get a newspaper
reminded me of the teacher I would miss
said would you like a lift
why not I said still no bus maybe
they had stopped running
he was looking for a newspaper
he said and a place to get coffee
then he asked where I'd been
to a writing class and with friends I said
oh he said I used to write a lot too
but it was not the flash
of the 12 inch knife nor his
arm pulling me
by the throat pulling
me down against
him but the sudden
shift of the world
as if the moon too
had just exploded
hail Mary kicking
full of grace no longer
believing but our Father
kicking the door who art
in heaven the street
lamps swimming

in the fog scream
and I'll kill you
a knife is always
loaded my head swimming
against his thigh
his arm locked
against my throat
the knife flashing hey
I said if I chattered
maybe I could disarm him
hey don't you have a girlfriend
a nice young man like you
the street lamps no longer
swam but dark
shapes probably trees
hid the moon he stopped
are you going to kill me
maybe
the knife
still at my throat as he
lifted my sweater groped
my breasts before
spending himself
if I had been
breathing I would
have been merely bored
so far I had survived
but if I jumped out now
now he was spent what
was in the park
was surely worse
wordlessly he locked
his arm again
around my throat
pulled me down and
no longer trees but fog a few
stars swam and then
he let go
shit he hissed
sit up it's the
goddamn cops
car lights flashed
scream and I'll kill you
the knife was on the floor now
I was rigid could
see waves car lights
flashed again

then the cops drove on
he reversed
and drove east
the knife
still on the floor
both his hands on the wheel
well he said
as suddenly again
thank you for not telling
those cops anything
now I'll take you home
you're so tight he said
I'd like to solve
your sex problems and I knew
I'd survive this night
he drove me home
my parents were asleep
but when I woke
and told them my father
turned over and my mother got
up and said what
do you expect
being out alone at night

MICHAEL McCLURE

THE DEATH OF KIN CHUEN LOUIE

NOW, ON THE DAY BEFORE MY DAUGHTER'S
TWENTY-FIRST BIRTHDAY,
ON THE AFTERNOON OF HER PARTY,
I REVISIT THE SCENE OF THE DEATH
of Kin Chuen Louie.
He too was between twenty and twenty-one.
The newspapers called him
a smalltime extortionist.
But what are we all but small
time extortionists in the
proportionless
universe?
(I am in awe of the thought
of the coolness and sureness
of his assassin.)
Twelve days ago, on the Festival
of the Lord Buddha, shortly
after two in the afternoon,
Kin Chuen Louie left his flat
on Kearny Street.
Louie's young, long-haired murderer,
in black jacket and army pants,
waited with a .380
Walther automatic pistol holding
fourteen bullets. Kin Chuen Louie,
spotting his assailant, leaped
into his bright red Plymouth Fury.
The murderer stepped
to the driver's side and fired a shot
into Louie. Louie started the ignition
and slammed into reverse.
His foot stuck on the accelerator.
The car, propelled backward with great
force, jammed between
a building and a white car
parked there—knocking loose shards
of red brick painted over with beige.
The murderer stepped quickly

to the passenger side of the trapped
and roaring car and fired seven bullets
through the windshield
into a tight pattern on the head and neck
of Louie. A ninth shot missed,
going finger-deep
into brick. The killer
fled a few yards, turned at the corner,
and disappeared down Sonoma Alley.
A moment later,
we arrived on the empty street
and looked through
shattered glass
at the young Chinese man—
blood pouring out of the holes
in his head—slumped over
on his side. It was like the close-up
in a Sam Peckinpah movie.
He was completely relaxed
—finally and almost pleasantly limp
and serene—wearing an army jacket
and grubby levis...a slender, handsome,
clean-cut face with short hair boyishly
hanging in his eyes above
the dime-size bullet holes.
The blood pouring onto the seat covers
was a thick, reddish vermillion.
There was a peaceful, robbe-grilletish,
dim light inside the car.
The shattered window was like
a frosted spider web.
Either death is beautiful to see
—or we learn the esthetic
of death from films. BUT I do know
that our physical, athletic body,
a thing of perfect loops, and secret
and manifest
dimensions and breathings of consciousness
and unconsciousness, emanates
rainbows and actions,
and black flowers
and
it is there
to bear us through this world
and to kiss us goodbye at the doorstep
of any other.

I praise Everything-That-Is
for that blessing.
I drink chrysanthemum
tea in his memory.
Candied ginger, scented with licorice
from Hong Kong,
is on my breath.

I know each death

shall be as fine as his is.

"WE ARE ADDICTED TO OUR PERSONALITIES"

WE ARE ADDICTED TO OUR PERSONALITIES.
(I AM!)
What pleasure then to let it go, and slide
away from all the pain.
But
then
WE ARE NOTHING
is the cry—
and that is right.

LOKI GETS THE LAST LAUGH.

We are hollow snakes in nowhere.
If the tanner comes
and takes the skin
then what is left
is the frost giant's grin
reflected on a glacier.

BLACKNESS
splits into two ravens,
Thought and *Memory*.
They
fly
forward
and settle on our shoulders.

The well stares up at us with one eye
and a trillion-billion facets
stir when the hazelnut
of personality drops in.

AND
THEN
THE SALMON LEAPS
AND EATS THE MAYFLY!

Sounds of motorcycles grinding on the peaks.
Feel of Autumn in the air.
Russet ripples.

Maid Quiet walking on the leafy forest floor.

THE CAVE WHERE CHILDREN PLAY
BENEATH THE GIANT STUMP.

And
—like art nouveau—
the black wings
make weird silhouettes
that we see between.
They tell me everything has a name
because the universes rub together.

An apple brushing on a feather.

MICHAEL KOCH

POEM

/i lodge in you like a bullet. i lick my fingers that undressed you.
i have just enough time for nothing & just enough time for you.
i shy away from my breath. my bones mend. my heart is skyblue.
sudden noises leap out of my hair. i sigh like a child with a moustache.
i send my mistaken identity greetings. i use love like a chain saw.
i taste my teeth.
Break into my house & take me. i wait for you, a vacant room filling
with water, groaning like swollen wood.

/she wrap jasmine up, she keep cool black gloves.
strangled blossoms follow her.

she hid in the barn. she hide her charm.

knuckles under, bottoms up, we love low as roots, stumps split
                                        by lightning

/the grapes have terrible faces.
love strikes.
the circle tightens its angles.

our chests heave with senseless exertion.
love, that permeates, mutates us.

/night lacks light.
gravity locks itself
in.

o hot influenza borne
on the wind, o mother of hand-
painted eggs.
yr serial numbers are
my entire body.
        i subtract heartbeats.
        i add thumbs.
everywhere the perfect fractions
                of love

/You're the space between raindrops in a tor-
rential rain,

a headline in a foreign language:

the presidential palace is burning!

FERNANDO ALEGRÍA

THE DISAPPEARED WILL INHERIT THE EARTH

But the ones who disappeared begin to come back
they come back in taxicabs, in ambulances
in vans and trucks
by way of the river and through the park
rolling downhill
Ortiz with his lean face
appears in an elevator
Soria rises again from the depths
driving his official Fiat
they come burning into the streets
crying their voiceless words
forefingers pointing at the dictator's liver
They come out wiser at night
bloodless, incredulous, long
like the hour they leave behind
they make alarming signals
they come running making no noise
as if the fog erased them from the pavement
shoulder to shoulder these protesting dead
with holes in their heads and their chests
jumping about the city on invisible crutches

And the disappeared appeared again
from the helicopters to the rocks
from the rocks to the helicopters
from the sea to the bottomless times
from the vaults of banks and churches
from wicker baskets and steel cages
from septic tanks and electrical hangars
from the holds of ships, trains and airplanes
in buses, on foot, opening coffins with their fingernails
dusty, bloody, carrying their worms and their embalming fluids

They show up running, shouting, pounding on doors and windows
disturbing death with pots full of bones
and they follow the general and put him in bed
they sit at his table, they vomit blood on his knees
they are his retinue at mass, they stick to his shoulders
they fly beside his helicopter fluttering shrewdly

Then the disappeared started putting bombs on
streetcorners
sand in motors
they close up shop, businesses go broke, prices go up
they hide the copper and go out on strike

The disappeared keep on shooting, my general,
they leave their dead behind

The dictator says: The country is under control
I govern the people shot full of holes
trampled in the tomb as the bell tolls

But the day finally came when the disappeared
took over
they declared themselves in the majority
and came up out of the mines, from the seaports and mountains
from cities, villages, islands and deserts
out of the sea and the sky
rushing with their remains of mortar and brick
with a strong stride, led by a skeleton
burned, broken, rotted away
brandishing spears, firing machineguns
wrapped in tear gas
and beating their drums, they raised their flags
their walls and scaffolds
they dealt out justice kindly as cadavers
and put up history's last monument:
an invisible arch to the general who vanished

ELEGY FOR ORLANDO LETELIER

Compañero,
you had found the just course
when the reefs rose up,
you saw the sky of our country dawning
when the fires grew confused
with the red flowers of our springtime.

Today in a strange land the leaves are turning gold
and the twilights shorten

the blue hour is spreading over the secret country of victory.

On the carpet on their knees next to the old copper coffin
your children's shadow is watching your arrival
their face beside yours
tenderly like votive candles
speaking with the sun about to be born.

Unforeseen banner
unarmed soldier
your inner security folded its wings
and so you've come to the strait gate.
Beautiful hero who suddenly appeared in September rain
you conduct the powers of life and of death
you know the honor of silence and the racket of birds
in the fallen trees.
You live.
Ambassador of my wounded people.
Ambassador of the poor.
Ambassador of the heroes of the resistance.
Today you rise out of the homeland's cold solitude
and return in the love of comrades,
the people's chalk writes your name on the sky.

You breathe with a rough voice in your stone guitar
you make a steel plate with your own hands
and begin eating the prisoners' moon,
you give every life you have
and wake up beating in the heart of Chile.
You're the motion of peace and our oceans' backbone
you move in the mystery of our rainy forests
and in the dawning light of our old deserts.

Compañero,
now you're the man who'll never travel alone.
Lord of the struggle.
Red gentleman of *cuecas* and snowy poplars,
the great and the humble go with you,
the silent passengers in Chile's fog,
the velvet compañera
gathers you in her arms like a sheaf of fresh wheat.

Defend us:
give us your strength to fight and to be reborn with you.

NOCTURNE

A peasant mother to her child

Sometimes we are drawn toward the earth
by what is most hidden between our hands.
A child of white lilies and wheat
a light lost and found among paths
where the leaves are asleep like stars.
Sometimes and who knows only once and never more
we make sense of the strange way we are watched by stones,
little white moist moons moving across the ground
signaling to us with their flags of dust.
Your hand in mine,
a moment in the world which lowers its ear
and settles down to listen to your breath on my neck,
the stars still, the sky lit up by the rubbing
of wings in search of sleep, all
the water, given to its celestial arrogance,
you and I grazed by a naked tenderness,
like the footstep long since gone that's given back
the nightingale its story among gardenias.
And I know you've fallen asleep, but time will open
for you alone among what spins the night
and stops, what understands us and flies away
sometimes and who knows
only once and never more.

—poems translated by Stephen Kessler

LUCHA CORPI

LETTER TO ARTURO

Darling,
the ants have invaded
the bread-box
and parade with a coffin
of bread on their shoulders.

The bluejays are getting drunk
on wild blackberries,
they're all in a row on the fence
celebrating the arrival of summer.

The snails are staying out of the sun
stretching like cats
under the microfronds
of the violets.
(Did you know that snails' houses
have no windows?—
Only a door.)

I sit down in front of an afternoon
that is languidly
counting its minutes
and listen to its emptiness.

You've hardly left
and already I miss the light
caress of your hands
on my hair,
and your laughter and your tears,
and all your questions
about seas,
moons and deserts.

And all my poems
are tying themselves together
in my throat.

ROMANCE OF THE LITTLE GIRL

Beside the dollhouse
little Sonia plays
at being a porcelain lady.

And the point of a lie
begins to sink
into the heart of the morning.

OBSOLETARIUM

I suffer when I look at
my imprisoned feet.

My little toe
a victim of progress
begs me to let it go
back to being
that little pig
that went for a walk.

And I hardly dare
tell it that these days
being a pilgrim is
the business of ants.

—*poems translated by Catherine Rodriguez-Nieto*

AARON SHURIN

from MULTIPLE HEART

The figure of falling, falling forward, the figure kneeling, hands on dirty concrete, palms down, or the forehead touching grass. An agon of reconciliation: submission, the rapture of falling. Who captures you forewarned, a tongue's embrace, the wagon or welcome mat for real, to fill you with what you failed to realize, the God grants the God mercy to pardon the God.

*   *   *

regenerate is off the body's own sickness twist
among the *poudres* of tranquility   the spasm
releases its beads, unsprung, the rosary
held tight revealed as rose garden

So the moment opens wide we call
present is blossom here & there in field   return
again & gain to process
dispersed

*   *   *

Before the acquisition we had to dismantle the wall, which did not fall (as she said) nevertheless was hung with monstrosities. And these we keep in corners under covers   my Baby was sitting by the refrigerator in white undershirt dazed after sex, glazed with lotion, swimming inside sea extended post-act like smell. He tried to hide in a quilt. I made him quit the quilt. His wall was overhung, I said Baby come into the light where my actual love is shining   then I saw that what he was lovely effortless in hairdo accidental slant of strands impeccable fall

*   *   *

Not to be beholden to anticipation
either in length or breadth, breath of ashes
equal to any infusion of sustenance,
the spore regales the fungus with tales of air
Certainly there is any sure way, in loping movement
as flash, & the ineptitude of synapse or
inevitable flow of old silence calls forward
as it will, the will to forward

that, as it should be, determines exact
juncture, fall of foot, root, wing, or bone
Some are many & some alone or none to
call the heart a heart, spade a spade, jeweled
with precision each, when get to it, fruitless seed
you thought was broken blossoming out of dead wood

*   *   *

and love shall love shall love shall over all incumbency dominion, idle
caresses rose-lipped & minds locked fierce eyes piercing. I have had all & it
shall, has taken me anew   recumbence in fire, licked salt, bushes, bruised,
swollen tips, the drift my flesh takes is thought's deepest desiring   sighs
well up as intellection springs. Love shall be called forward called all, being
now inside hegemony among each blushing word the truest touch of
tongue's frail blessing

*   *   *

restricted in no sense wise or not, tears running down face at mere mention
of her name, his glory, (my Hera)—this was, as was, long ago, I was reading,
she had chunky solid cracked the clunky case, refracted speech, and so she
had she did. It made her great. & only one among the ones before who stand
before in largeness, bulk, extravagant vastness we meekly seek to emulate
in song. How stabbed he was, for me, because my master called me slave.
How thoroughly, I said, deliciously, I slave to master.

*   *   *

O that river song green came through again body bountiful, that lay back in the arms of water I also called breast, beautiful to merely look, mere looking raised to real sight, floating without acceleration or goal, baking little cookie of self in shell evaporating—tender thing. Inside the book the river runs into itself again again. I took my own self to the headlands, crawled along the dusty ground, ground my bare back into the dust.   Who was there? He was. With me. We swam away together. O that river, flung in ribbons, ran, runs, will run, the rungs of pleasure ascend midday as if water flowing upwards flew

RAVING #16

Dammit   you fit!
no ideal
construction I make
has the power to nestle in
like you do,   bird's nest,   cradle.
A fact
either proves a theory

or develops its own. My arms
want to shriek out:
        one grabbing
        the other stiffing: Stop!

our stomachs rub together.
those little hairs as I stroke
the planed wood of yr back.
A body
either proves what you have to say

or just goes ahead anyway.
my heart is in my heart.

LESLIE SIMON

THE END

my father's pipe hangs out of the car ash tray. he is dead three days. i am driving his car. i look down. it stares up. like he's still alive. my father smoked three packs of cigarettes a day. he tried a pipe. to cut down. you might say he was an oral person. i come from an oral family. smoke and stories fill the air. you might say i have a rich oral tradition.

hand fingers smoking stick. carries fire to mouth. lips suck. i will swallow this smoke if it kills me. o pray, let it kill me. this slow suicide for love. something. anything. in my mouth. lips form. teeth grab words. fast. some say "take three deep breaths. it will slow you down." i don't want to slow down. this rhythm is a music you must take in the bargain, this obsession i trade in. my lovers will like it or they will leave. many leave. some stay. we play. all day.

i want to take you fast. i get wet quick. it is not feminine. i can't help this. "take three long breaths." but what if after the second long breath you are gone. you see. this is a race. i stumble over words to get you in my arms. when you leave me i think you are dead. this is a false power born from a worried mind. this is a girl who lost her father in the middle of adolescent fantasy. when you leave me. i think i have killed you. your tongue hanging from a still hot ash tray.

the presence of death in our passageways. the fear of deformity, maiming, damage. a drive into the unknown.

love.

the great scientists reveal love and death are old driving partners. death sits gunshot. jumps out to unlock the gate. love drives the truck through. death swings the gate shut. jumps in the cab. love pulls them both into heaven.

if you don't believe this story, you will smash through the gate alone, destroying the truck, love, and yourself. it is destiny. history manifests itself in each generation.

cement is in my passageways. it is in my blood. is this a twentieth century perversity. or do i fly over cities, flapping my tincan wings, howling to the spirits, begging them not to abandon centers of populace. do i fly with some nineteenth century mission glazed on my eyes. or rather is it the coming century's vision and nightmare. collapse and revival.

flowers shake in the wind.

rusty lover. flake of iron. what age was it that didn't have its souvenir of love.

TAKING BESSIE TO MANCHESTER

(aprés Stein)

Redness. the air of every. it filled her heart. that red.
she was struck. the speed (the deed, a reed) at which. the
notion. reached her brain.

rock in hock. o shock. the lock. the lock. oh cock. oh.
oh. mock.

at which the red filled her heart. the Redness. that thing.
simple spread. sandwich bread. red fill/ at will/ her heart/
that part. refrain, disdain. eat it. Now.

which rock? oh hock, not to mock.

and still it was, handily, handily. Oh Christ. you too? we
two.

I do. I do. I do. We three is me. don't you see? the cock
the sock the lock.

Did Rock. Did Rock. Did Rock.

Taking Bessie to Manchester.

HAROLD NORSE

REMEMBERING PAUL GOODMAN

1

As I cross a windy streetcorner
waiting for a bus
that never comes
in the wind and the rain
I remember
how Paul walked
with a shaggy dog trot
and half-shy smile
pipesmoking
toward a drunken party
where he ran
to hard young bodies
and handsome faces
tho' loss of balance disgusted him.
People fell
into the bathtub, smashed,
and Paul stood as if amazed
at the madness of crowds.
And I recall once
when he stood at his window
sight-translating
Our Lady of the Flowers
how his blue intellectual eye
kindled suddenly
at a passing navy ass
and as he brought a criminal beauty
out of the French language
a revolver went off in his mouth
releasing
orgasms
of
light.

2

Now he does not exist
those parties are gone

the nights the lovers
gone
only the feelings remain
another here
another now
the written word will survive
somehow
in somebody's memory
this is the truth of poetry
to make it new each lifetime
Pound's gold standard of letters
Goodman's bitter faith

I write to make myself real
from moment to moment
how else do I know
I exist
if I didn't I'd go
mad with emptiness
and boredom I confess
Paul Goodman
helped us live
in the present
tense

3

Strange to hear your voice
disembodied on tape
lecturing at universities
over the air (and you're dead and gone)
less bitter than 20 years ago
some say more bitter
but you were diffident then
and shy
needing the sweet turned neck
and the ear of the young
you pursued love and fame
for what? towards what?

Lonely old Orpheus
Romantic woodsy Wordsworth
anarchist Shelley of coldwater flats
on your bicycle over the bridges
loving the pastoral urban scene
dashing to handball courts for quickies

```
              blowing the boys
        in parking lots and doorways
        with Puerto Ricans on stoops
            secret jackoffs on East Side roofs
        with shepherds of chance on streetcorners
            among traffic horns and coffee smells
              smells of urine and sperm in sacred latrines
                bus stations, bars, penny arcades
                42nd Street grope movies
            whiskey and smoke and kisses
O Empire City!
```

```
            Soul-brother Socrates
            tugs at your elbow—
                Catullus declaims: Paedicabo ego vos
                                et irrumabo!
            You lived in sad neglect
                till late success brought dollars
                gray hair & heart attacks—
              your son Matthew dead at 20
                your wife Sally once applecheeked
                    growing old. . . .
```

You wrote *The Facts of Life*
and we read our poems and joked
and met Edith Sitwell, noble scarecrow dyke
with birdlike mask
and Jean Cocteau signed copies of OPIUM
and *The Eagle Has Two Heads*
        saying
            "These English words...these are not my words...."
and flirted with me
and you were jealous
biting the stem of your pipe as if it were the pin of a grenade....
And when I said you were our Sartre everyone looked uncomfortable
        in 1945
but when you died the other day
a famous critic called you that
and I bought *Hawkweed* for a dollar
and read those kinky poems again
—a voice unique and personal
caught as in rock for future years!

4

Patchen's slow death of bitter pain
        Jarrell stepped in front of a car

Sylvia Plath stuck her head in the oven
      Delmore Schwartz OD'd on booze
O'Hara struck by a beach buggy
Berryman highdived from a bridge waving
      Blackburn went by cigarettes
         & Goodman forgot his pills
      give & take a few years
these are the poets of my generation
      Paul's poems kept growing bleaker
         with indignation & rage
      with every sleepless night
that went without love as age crept up
      who's next? the pattern's old
freaks of the western wilderness
between the bughouse & the bar
American poets live their lives
      some starve tho' you may not hear it
      others vanish into academe
to sugarcoat their hell, grow dull
      Paul with his "pretty farm"
tried the Horatian life, it didn't work
      in a black flag he draped his love
tobacco, wrong food, loneliness
      stopped his heart the American way

5

Writing *The Glass Menagerie* was no cinch, Tennessee.

"It's only a potboiler!" he said. "Wouldn't you rather see my poems?"

Julian Beck spoke of Gertrude Stein and the revolution of feeling.
He raised black flags in hell
and threatened the world with peace and saintly patience.

Jimmy Baldwin emerged from 5 a.m. mist into neon cafeterias
with watchcap and desperado eyes
placing his naked soulscript in my hands, his negritude,
and we had to choose bars carefully.

Paul Goodman sat on my floor listening to Auden—
their first meeting—both thought they were Shelley....

Ginsberg high in the subway, red kerchief round his neck,
recited Rimbaud in eerie dawn of 1944
drowned by the IRT, the flood of words across the aisle from me

and then departed for mad mindmusic after we greeted the future.

The '40s...death, sex and war...sailors everywhere...
jukebox romance of South Sea guitars....
we cruised the salty seas of love
in what seemed unending youth....

I recall it all
through a scrim of decades
and broken love affairs
and rubble of dead friendships.
Paul was not sentimental:
"I do not eulogize dead men," he said.

I find that fitting.

San Francisco, 1972

CAROL TARLEN

WELFARE RIGHTS

Don't never tell nobody
you're on welfare
        not even your
best friend he still
might dump scorn
on your face and hands
        thinkin behind your
smile you're a degenerate
lay-about sloth
            dog shit and
you don't even own no
dog not bein able to
purchase pet food
            with foodstamps
no baby don't even
        whisper welfare
specially when you hitch
a ride with a pressed
            and shiney pro-
fessional man or a
laborin dude with
grease stains on his pants
and they just have to
know how you live
as if your stretched out
raggedy thumb didn't already
                say it all
and so you grunt
I get these checks in
the mail on the 1st and
15th of each month
and then by some cosmic
consciousness or just ordin-
ary street sense they
decide you're desperate
for anything and they
leer and rub their
scorpion legs against yours
offerin $10 or 400 dependin

on what they're wearin
and you got to be polite and
innocent and lower your eyes
           real sugary
just like your mama
taught you mutterin
No Thank You Sir
when you're burnin up
inside and your finger-
nails just achin for
     some blood

LAURA FELDMAN

IN MY SUITE AT THE PLAZA

A boat in the bay and around
a recurrent dream
adolescence on a field trip
locked in a men's bathroom with toilets
spit into the wind: Alcatraz
overflowing he cuts the woman off at the corner
machine gun kelly
almost running her over
no escaping of digging the way out
I followed him around the corner
salt weathered sea cement
into a parking lot
with spoons no longer inescapable
no hurry going nowhere as I
but the fierce tides and freezing water
slapping him in the face repeatedly
jack la lane swam it many times
he said I'm only trying to get there
once towing a rowboat with his teeth
challenge continually changed him
but those boys didn't have physiques
the result was a man totally connected
vitamin deficiencies
to his times while campaigning he shook
three of them working in the admin. building
hands until his hands bled
wrote themselves free from Washington, D.C.
that's what happened
a seal swims by
he has the kind of hands that are fleshy
noon notices
clumsy incapable of coordination for malice
they chase each other around the deck
absent of courage but dangerous
oh to not be young again
and heavy by accident
pretend to shoot seagulls the boys
all the same

the girls shriek and shriek
reagan offers to drop the force in Europe
a man sits quietly decomposing in the back seat
mommy isn't it lucky he doesn't have it on his face
extreme permutations gravitate to the gothams
the yellow cab jerks to a stop
everybody's gone surfin
a mummy bounds forward in the back seat
pulled in like maggots to
falling back as the cab jerks on
sucked in as in undertow
the backwash of most potent emotional businessmen
people standing in doorways for long periods
the bear had bitten two people already
the lady he bit on the arm
police reported that both the bear and the woman
had been drinking
have no excuse must show papers
one had a fascination for locks
unfortunately my hands were in the way
the other had a fear
sometimes all in one night
sometimes all in one cup
which one do you think escaped?
to work with children
he gave me a fork and knife for my soup
and said finally
I tried the fork
the movie was a lie
maybe jesus walked on water
bonnie never smoked a cigar
but it didn't work
she was only mugging
we had a falling out over shoelaces
clyde came from the wrong side of the tracks
I grew so tired of cockroaches
and told his mother never again
I began killing the babies with my hands
I just had a fascination with locks
and drowning the big ones
you, with the banana, come
someone said they can swim
that's not part of my job
in the dream always trying to explain
I once had a cockroach named Tad

JACK MICHELINE

I APPLIED FOR MENTAL ASSISTANCE

Man does not want to share the wealth
He wants to keep it all to himself
Fear again that runs the wheel of the world
Locks
Keys
Engines
And the Church
And the dogs of the world on chains
Here Snooky
Hey doggy
Hey world
The meat rack on Polk Street without soul
And the psychiatrist I met at the 1232 bar wants to work inside
the system tearing down the old buildings
and putting up the white
white cemetery walls
If thoughts and words were guns
I would have an army marching across the world
An army of love and joy without shame or guilt
I would take the military men and make them clowns in the zoo
And the feeding of the hungry
The responsibility of the soybean brokers
And what it comes down to
The crux and crucible of it all
The power of light and spirit
Love lights gleaming
Across the bridges of nations
Paranoia thrown down
And Macho turned into dwarfs
Real estate into art studios
And football stadiums into orgies
I have applied for mental assistance because I am insane
I told the shrink I was Prince Bulganin
And I want to share love and joy and beauty
and believe the innocence of birds and dogs and children
It is eight in the morning and the engines are racing across town
And children are going to school
And the Nut is nobody right and nobody's wrong
And each one has his or her own truth

Here in the stone citadels of my Mongolian America
And the hospitals and prisons and groans
The bird does not compromise with the air
I have walked the street of my land out of my head
And the cemeteries are full of good people
And it's just the living that's fucked up
And those who have not walked with me will never understand
I see love lights across the universe
Shoe shine
Shoe shine
Shoe shine
Shoe shine!

THE EYES OF CARUSO
AND THE LEGS OF A BALLET DANCER

It was one of those rare nights
The kid had wild eyes
He was down on his luck
The truck stop was crowded and crazy
His name was Salem
He needed a place to stay
Two days in the city from L.A.
He was sixteen or seventeen or nineteen
He was human and a rare flower
A fruit
A lady
A Drag Queen
A cock sucker
A beautiful boy man child
He shared my bed
For one night
In my skinny furnished room
It took him a half hour to put his makeup on
He smiled
He sang me a song
I kissed him with my tongue
He blew me before he said goodbye
With the eyes of Caruso
And the legs of a ballet dancer

San Francisco, February, 1975

SUMMER EVENING IN HARLEM

you hear the voices singing
you hear the horn that cries

Sophie got a headache
Arnold he done died

most people they just walkin
some going for a ride

stoops full of dreamers
bar rooms full of lies

that dollar bill done got us
till the day we die

the Lord's comin preacher Willie says
the Lord's comin pretty soon

still the voices singing
still the horn that cries

Sophie got a headache
Arnold he done died

that dollar bill done got us
till the day we die

1956

PAT PARKER

MOVEMENT IN BLACK

Movement in Black
movement in Black
can't keep em back
movement in Black

I

They came in ships
from a distant land
bought in chains
to serve the man

I am the slave
that chose to die
I jumped overboard
& no one cried

I am the slave
sold as stock
walked to and fro
on the auction block

They can be taught
if you show them how
they're strong as bulls
and smarter than cows.

I worked in the kitchen
cooked ham and grits
seasoned all dishes
with a teaspoon of spit.

I worked in the fields
picked plenty of cotton
prayed every night
for the crop to be rotten.

All slaves weren't treacherous
that's a fact that's true
but those who were
were more than a few.

Movement in Black
Movement in Black
Can't keep em back
Movement in Black

II

I am the Black woman
& i have been all over
when the colonists
fought the British
i was there
i aided the colonist
i aided the British
i carried notes,
stole secrets,
guided the men
& nobody thought
to bother me
i was just a
Black woman
the britishers lost
and I lost,
but I was there
& i kept on moving

I am the Black woman
& i have been all over
i went out west, yeah
the Black soldiers
had women too,
& i settled the land,
& raised crops & children,
but that wasn't all
i hauled freight,
& carried mail,
drank plenty whiskey
shot a few men too.
books don't say much

about what I did
but I was there
& i kept on moving.

I am the Black woman
& i have been all over
up on platforms & stages
talking about freedom
freedom for Black folks
freedom for women
In the civil war too
carrying messages,
bandaging bodies
spying and lying
the south lost
& i still lost
but i was there
& i kept on moving

I am the Black woman
& I have been all over
I was on the bus
with Rosa Parks
& in the streets
with Martin King
I was marching
and singing
and crying
and praying
I was with SNCC
& i was with CORE
I was in Watts
when the streets
were burning
I was a panther
in Oakland
In new york
with N.O.W.
In San Francisco
with gay liberation
in D.C. with
the radical dykes
yes, I was there
& i'm still moving

movement in Black
movement in Black
can't keep em back
movement in Black

III

I am the Black woman

I am Bessie Smith
singing the blues
& all the Bessies
that never sang a note

I'm the southerner
who went north
I'm the northerner
who went down home

I'm the teacher
in the all Black school
I'm the graduate
who cannot read

I'm the social worker
in the city ghetto
I'm the car hop
in a delta town

I'm the junkie with a jones
I'm the dyke in the bar
I'm the matron at county jail
I'm the defendant with nothin' to say.

I'm the woman with 8 kids
I'm the woman who didn't have any
I'm the woman who poor as sin
I'm the woman who's got plenty.

I'm the woman who
raised white babies &
taught my kids to
raise themselves.

movement in Black
movement in Black
can't keep em back
movement in Black

IV

Roll call, shout em out

Phyliss Wheatley
Sojourner Truth
Harriet Tubman
Frances Ellen Watkins Harper
Stagecoach Mary
Lucy Prince
Mary Pleasant
Mary McLeod Bethune
Rosa Parks
Coretta King
Fannie Lou Hammer
Marion Anderson
& Billies
& Bessie
sweet Dinah
A-re-tha
Natalie
Shirley Chisolm
Barbara Jordan
Patricia Harris
Angela Davis
Flo Kennedy
Zora Neale Hurston
Nikki Giovanni
June Jordan
Audre Lorde
Edmonia Lewis
and me
and me
and me
and me
and me

& all the names we forgot to say
& all the names we didn't know
& all the names we don't know, yet.

movement in Black
movement in Black
Can't keep em back
movement in Black

V

I am the Black woman
I am the child of the sun
the daughter of dark
I carry fire to burn the world
I am water to quench its throat
I am the product of slaves
I am the offspring of queens
I am still as silence
I flow as the stream

I am the Black woman
I am a survivor
I am a survivor
I am a survivor
I am a survivor
I am a survivor

Movement in Black.

NELLIE WONG

FROM A HEART OF RICE STRAW

Ma, my heart must be made of rice straw,
the kind you fed a fire in Papa's home village
so Grandma could have hot tea upon waking,
so Grandma could wash her sleepy eyes. My heart
knocks as silently as that LeCoultre clock
that Papa bought with his birthday money.
It swells like a baby in your stomach.

Your tears have flooded the house, this life.
For Canton? No, you left home forty years ago
for the fortune Papa sought in Gum San.
In Gold Mountain you worked side by side
in the lottery with regular pay offs
to the Oakland cops. To feed your six daughters
until one day Papa's cousin shot him.

I expected you to fly into the clouds, wail
at Papa's side, but you chased cousin instead.
Like the cops and robbers on the afternoon radio.
It didn't matter that Papa lay bleeding.
It didn't matter that cousin accused Papa
of cheating him. You ran, kicking
your silk slippers on the street, chasing
cousin until you caught him, gun still in hand.
My sister and I followed you, crying.

If cousin had shot you, you would have died.
The cops showed up and you told them how cousin
gunned Papa down, trusted kin who smoked
Havana cigars after filling his belly with rice
and chicken in our big yellow house.

Papa lay in his hospital bed, his kidney removed.
Three bullets out. They couldn't find the last
bullet. A search was made, hands dove into Papa's
shirt pocket. A gold watch saved Papa's life.

Ma, you've told this story one hundred times.
The cops said you were brave. The neighbors said

you were brave. The relatives shook their heads,
the bravery of a Gold Mountain woman unknown
in the old home village.

The papers spread the shooting all over town.
One said Papa dueled with his brother like
a bar room brawl. One said it was the beginning
of a tong war, but that Occidental law
would prevail. To them, to the outside,
what was another tong war, another dead Chinaman?

But Papa fooled them. He did not die
by his cousin's hand. The lottery closed down.
We got food on credit. You wept.
I was five years old.

My heart, once bent and cracked, once
ashamed of your China ways.
Ma, hear me now, tell me your story
again and again.

FOR MY SISTER WHOSE NAME, AMONG OTHERS, IS COURAGE

Who is she? She lies on the hospital bed.
She vomits, weary from chemotherapy,
fragile as spring narcissus.

She is my sister. I look at her deeply, quietly.

She serves an ace on the tennis court,
runs her opponent ragged.
She organizes a festival, year after year,
to celebrate Asian Pacific American heritage.

She rises, goes to work.
She serves pancakes and coffee
to customers at the Great China.
She types for Milen's Jewelers,
waits on tables at Plands Restaurant,
serves trays of cocktails at Tiki Bob's.

Meanwhile, after she cooks dinner
for her husband and children,
at midnight she cooks and serves chow mein
to her mother-in-law's friends
who play round after round of mah jongg.

Who is she? This woman who fights back
with every breath, this woman who is my sister,
and I love her.

Her hair grows back.
Fragility is not her nature,
not this sister who raised three children,
this sister who stretches and runs,
who skis, bowls, supervises an office
for the Oakland Unified School District.

She, whose hand links mine,
as we run on the grass at Lake Merritt,
drink our parents' homemade lemonade
served from an aluminum stew pot,
as we hunt for our lost baby brother
as we picnic beneath the redbud, laughing,
holding back our thick long hair.

She is Leslie   ai ng nui   fifth daughter
Thlom Gawk Ngon   three-corner eye
Ah Lessalee   Dragon Teen   Cotton Ball Queen
She is Lai Ying   Beautiful Eagle
breathing   strong   living

SUSAN GRIFFIN

GRANDMOTHER

After so long
she died.
Eighty years old,
they said,
"She had a long life;
she didn't suffer
when she went."
That's not the point.
But what is?
We should have all got
together
after all of these years,
strung out all over
the state, but she
would not have
a funeral and was
burned. She was
my Grandmother,
held me on her lap
when I was young.
I wept on her
breast and combed her
white hair, and
loved her for the way
her arms knew
my pain. She taught me
to read, and brush my
teeth, iron my clothes,
scramble eggs,
spread jam on bread,
clean up crumbs from
all the tables, grind
meat, stifle laughs,
grit my teeth, say the
right thing,
shake hands, watch to see
if my slip was hanging, to
put my hair in a french roll
wear mascara and

use a lip brush,
file my nails, bathe in
oil. She saved little things for me.
Her things, she'd say,
"My things, let me show
you my things; don't
let a stranger
who doesn't know
their value, touch
my things." The crystal
polar bears, the
rose plates,
the chair we could never
sit in. I don't want them.
I want
my Grandmother
so we might
do what we
should have done
in life,
sit down together
drunk or tired and
worn down or crazy with
ecstasy, so we might
sit down together
and sing out our grief.

A WOMAN DEFENDING HERSELF EXAMINES HER OWN CHARACTER WITNESS

QUESTION: Who am I?
ANSWER: You are a woman.
Q. How did you come to meet me?
A. I came to meet you through my own pain and suffering.
Q. How long have you known me?
A. I feel I have known you since my first conscious moment.
Q. But how long really?
A. Since my first conscious moment—for four years.
Q. How old are you?
A. Thirty-one years old.
Q. Will you explain this to the court?

A. I was not conscious until I met you through my own pain and suffering.

Q. And this was four years ago?

A. This was four years ago.

Q. Why did it take you so long?

A. I was told lies.

Q. What kind of lies?

A. Lies about you.

Q. Who told you these lies?

A. Everyone. Most only repeating the lies they were told.

Q. And how did you find out the truth?

A. I did not. I only stopped hearing lies.

Q. No more lies were told?

A. Oh no. The lies are still told, but I stopped hearing them.

Q. Why?

A. My own feelings became too loud.

Q. You could not silence your own feelings any longer?

A. That is correct.

Q. What kind of woman am I?

A. You are a woman I recognize.

Q. How do you recognize me?

A. You are a woman who is angry.
You are a woman who is tired.
You are a woman who receives letters from her children.
You are a woman who was raped.
You are a woman who speaks too loudly.
You are a woman without a degree.
You are a woman with short hair.
You are a woman who takes her mother home from the hospital.
You are a woman who reads books about other women.
You are a woman whose light is on at four in the morning.
You are a woman who wants more.
You are a woman who stopped in her tracks.
You are a woman who will not say please.
You are a woman who has had enough.
You are a woman clear in your rage.
And they are afraid of you
I know
they are afraid of you.

Q. This last must be stricken from the record as the witness does not know it for a fact.

A. I know it for a fact that they are afraid of you.

Q. How do you know?

A. Because of the way they tell lies about you.

Q. If you go on with this line you will be instructed to remain silent.

A. And that is what they require of us.

MICHAEL MAYO

THE DAY AFTER

*for Joseph Lee Rykiel "who believed the end was near,
and so it came closer, drinking himself into wild turkey
oblivion, until he saw the light, and it was the hydrogen bomb."*

To what shall I compare the earth the day after nuclear exchange?
Shall I begin by counting the warheads as grains of sand, soon enough
    to fill all the beaches of cape cod?
Shall I begin by numbering the days to Armageddon and start counting
    backwards until I fall asleep?
Shall I begin by saying that bomb now wears the disguise of terrorist
    mailman, has all our addresses in his plutonium backpocket?
Shall I say that unlike human being bomb has never wanted to be
    alone, has gathered unto himself all the resources of Europe America
    and the Soviet Union?
Shall I say bomb has no need of human fixtures the waterfaucet the
    incandescent bulb the doorlatch, that he comes and goes as he pleases
    among the heads of state?
Shall I say that it was bomb thought up the appropriations poured the
    cement wired the electric circuits, that it is bomb repairs the B-52
    runways of nuclear oblivion?
Shall I say that bomb has been done without sexual relations, is fruitful
    and multiplies upon the face of the earth and is rising even now into
    the glory of the sky?
Shall I say then that bomb is god greater than Zeus Caesar Allah and
    Jehovah rolled into one, exacts his tribute into the hundreds of
    billions of dollars?
Shall I say bomb sits content in judgment at electromagnetic vanishing
    point of history, with a wink of his cosmic eye wishes us all
    good luck?
Shall I say bomb is eleventh and final plague upon the house of human-
    kind? Woe! Woe unto them who would step into his way!
One trident submarine has more explosive power than all armies in
    warfare history.
What plebiscite commissioned monstrosity?
What ivy league graduate signed his name to requisition form
    of megadeath?
Who broke champagne bottle against hull of apocalypse sea serpent?
What annapolis crackpot pandered congressional seal of approval?
What will good housekeeping have to say about the mess?
What crime great enough in the making to stir conscience of nation?

Who woke up in the middle of the night with this bright idea I want
   to know!
Shall I go on and say there is intelligent life in the universe
   that knows nothing of these plans and lives in peace
   O where are you now?
Shall I issue my appeal for help in some as yet unknown galactic
   tongue?
Shall I say they might be able to teach an old and dying species
   a new trick or two?
What odds, Jimmy the Greek?
Which roulette table, Las Vegas?
How to get from here to there?
Will secret service transport presidential entourage the day after by
   rickshaw?
Will soviet politburo have to walk to work?
How many tibetans on their way to marketplace when the big one
   rock n rolls the himalayas?
Will washington burn down the house to roast its russian bear?
How many flights down fire escape of empire state?
How far into the earth to protect the federal reserve board?
What ventilation system necessary for survival of human race?
O now I can foretell the silence of transatlantic cable.
O now I can foretell the yearning of silverware.
O now I can foretell the desperation of baby stroller.
O now I can hear the lament of whale song rolling over and over
   in its oceanic grave.
O now I can hear the death knell of church bell over the remaining
   outposts of the race.
O now I can measure the hope the day after in a teaspoon.
President of USA is compulsive gambler with humanity.
President of USA is thermonuclear junkie.
US economy needs plutonium fix to get itself going in the morning and
   out the door.
Secretary of Defense has needle marks from shooting strontium-90.
White House staff gets its kicks snorting enriched U235.
Congress speeding its brains on fissionable material.
Fortune 500 military-industrial complex has hopeless bellyache from
   guzzling radioactive waste soon will be shitting phosphorescent
   bricks!
Shall I now appeal to prurient interests and say that arms race obscene,
   worthy of expulsion from granite halls of senile and stammering
   Congress?
Shall I say forthright the National Security Council is drunk with
   power and demand a sobriety test and mandatory jail sentence?
Shall I introduce my disarmament idea to the intelligence agencies
   as the next great emancipator?
What amber wave of grain?

What purple mountain majesty?

What heavenly tenderness take hold in the American heartland to stem the tide of such madness?

O tell me how many generations henceforth can dance on the nosecone of a ballistic missile?

O tell me could the great houdini get out of the straightjacket of deterrence alive?

Does Europe like Garbo just want to be left alone?

What riddle will sphinx think up the next time around?

How many nuclear wolf alerts before unbelievable happens?

What alice in wonderland dare come back through the looking glass into this world the day after nuclear exchange?

Where will the spirit of christmas past go?

How far over the rainbow to escape the fallout?

    O scarecrow of the impossible ground zero!

    O tin man with your heart in your throat!

    O cowardly lion! Who will be king now?

    O Dorothy! How return home to irradiated Kansas?

    O wizard! What wicked magician let this one out of the trap door in Pandora's box?

I say now that it will take a million gandhis to bring peace to planet.

I say now it will take a million einstein brains to outwit diabolical brain of missile launch system.

I say now it will take four score and twenty seven generations to undo damage already done by bomb.

Hopelessness of the young thy name is bomb.

All the young born under the sign of bomb.

How to cope with premonition of the end of the world?

    So long until tomorrow, Lowell Thomas!

    One giant leap for mankind, Neil Armstrong!

    A penny saved is a penny earned, Ben Franklin!

    Some pigs are more equal than others, George Orwell!

    Strawberry fields forever, Lennon and McCartney!

    I shall return, Douglas MacArthur!

    All the news that's fit to print!

    Remember the Alamo!

    Peace is at hand!

    Mine eyes have seen the glory of the coming of the Lord!

    Anchors away, my boys, anchors away!

    Ashes, ashes, we all fall down!

POEMS FOR A SMALL PLACE TO REST

Footprints in the snow, I walk the other way

•

The waterwheel that turned and
turned, then rusted:
What dreams it has of spring rains

•

Glass jar with fireflies—
    Light enough for haiku

•

Heart that breaks so easily—Tell me, how is it the autumn
    geese find their way back?

•

My door unlocked for the evening:
I have made this allowance
for the burglar and his wife

•

Tonight I sleep without pajamas
the pillow snug between my legs
And dream all night of being with you

•

Tide goes out, we go across, clammers dig deeper

•

Why should we sleep with one
master the rest of our lives:
you poets, get out of bed
and make some decent tea

•

The bones of your hand in mine
that hold the worlds in place, oh yes!

•

Birds at dawn—
    I hear their cries—
        Awakening!

SONG OF THE LITTLE GIRL

That little girl went and sold
her heart to the wind.
Not enough laughter
under the big sky.

The little wind that stole
the heart of the girl
goes dancing by.

Look, how the trees shake
in the little hands of the wind
that stole the heart
of the girl.

Look, how tiny they are
against the big sky,
sailing away.

O see how the sky is stained red
with the heart of that little girl!

RAFAEL JESÚS GONZÁLEZ

DECLARATIVE

I have lived my life
stepping on carousing weeds,
occasionally tripping
on a flying bird.
   I have worshipped
   a sea behind the eyes
& swallowed stars
fermented in dead dreams—

   (asters of blood-bread
   steeped in nocturnal wine
   squeezed from spoiled sleep.)

I have said: I love
& laughed the world between the teeth—
   taken the thistle in the brain
   & fashioned tongue-roses
   from its purple pith.

I say I have spat thorns
& eaten fruit of dust—

   to live
            is to love
                     is to die

(& I have seen
the edges of my heart turn rust.)

WINDSONG FOR PRINCE HENRY'S DAUGHTER

Cuatro cosas tiene el hombre
que no sirven en la mar:
ancla, governalle y remos,
y miedo de naufragar.
                    Antonio Machado

        for Carmen

Take a sextant to watch the stars by
    & cut the firmament in sixths;
take an astrolabe
    (because it has a lovely name),
& bees' wax,
    not against the sirens' song
    you wouldn't want to miss,
but because you might want
    the smell of flowers
just for one moment on the wine-dark sea.

Take one secret word you'll want to roll
    & knead within your mind,
a few friends' names
    (to invoke the angels by),
& a small mirror
    scratched with this charm:

        there is one center to the universe
        & it moves to wherever you are.

GENE FOWLER

A FARTHER LOVE

for D.

I nestle into your breasts
brought together and made full as you
lie on your side and curve
your shoulders to hold me.
You hold my head
to your breasts
and I hear your voice again
tightened slightly into a brave neutrality
telling me of a time
still live in your heart,
of a new born son taken
into the hospital,
of your breasts aching and full,
of one who vowed to love you
unable to take these
laden tendernesses
into his hands and, in love, into
his mouth, unable to drink
the nectar we all first drink
to birthe the spring, the first spring
of our living, unable in love to drink
and in drinking allow your body its
life and being, unable
to draw from you the food that
left becomes poison and knife and
the loss that groans out of you into
all the nights
to darken the sea
washing rock strewn
beaches our species must
live upon.
I listen to the sob so deep in your voice
no other would hear
or listen for
in the far waves crashing
behind the calmed
telling. I brush the full curve of
your breasts with my lips—

a light down moves under my breath,
a lone hair bends before it
like a tree before wind,
and I pass my lower lip
over the soft fold of aureole.
I pray, now, that an old skill
from long before the beginnings of
memory will come into my lips
and tongue and jaw
that I might lie upon your breasts
as a father who tenderly leads
his daughter into love, where another
might, in alien roughness, frighten
her; as a lover might lie who draws his
lover into himself even as he enters her;
as a new born son will lie who takes
his own flesh from her
through the thrusting pink
umbilical offered
the free and mobile, the inheritors
of choice. My eyes grow wet
that I was not there when your
need closed upon you and nightmare
screamed through your dark
inside, but I smile within as I find
within you the still live need for this
touch, and I open my lips
and close them about this bud,
let my tongue ride below this blossom
as it bumps and holds to my mouth roof,
and an old skill
does rise and feel its way
through throat and jaw
and tongue.
Then, I feed again
in our oldest, oldest
way; I love you
in a way older than consciousness.
Above me I hear
soft croonings of someone free'd,
of something loosed
that is Earth's love
for humankind.

THE DIVINITY OF SHIT

Leaves to wipe with and others
to avoid—a lore of herbs
more important
than most.

The first making, the
original
craft.
It's learned in infancy, or up
the first several years
with lapses
and worse badges than hammer-smashed thumbs
and it is a craft,
or a sculpting
and chemistry, practiced
in dark lands.
A pressing to a gather, and
the giving, then
extraction, of
waters, just
a balance
of water.
Then, the reaching back, inward, to take
in folded wing,
and a carrying forth...

I'll know one more plateau of enlightenment
when I can hunker at
roadside, pants
down and pulled forward,
and drop
a single turd, well
made, and not
smell shame
in the methane and decay
that'll make Earth rich in her green-
gold alloys.

When I smell only methane, pure in its being
and past it what
was eaten
and what will grow and flourish in clean
winds flowing.

Then, in this land where food's so abundant
my shit is feast for sparrows
and other seekers of bits,
I can hunker down
at road's side
in wisdom.

RICHARD LORANGER

NIGHT BEAT

On nights that rock I am rock yes
are you my one-time love
it goes on I'm still beating blues
Cal on bass was the earth tonight
ooo how fine your hair
holds the smoke the din the invisible lurking
beat & that's fine too
it is quiet & my head
ooo my head is full
the wild whirl the yell the fog
& John's strum steady flowing chords
he was our blood a stream calm now foaming
tumbling up the progression holding the brink
then down down down under you felt it
tantalizing like death & life & laughing whirling
drunk like madness I'm drunk on your breasts
firm & warm yearning mother beauty cry of it cry
for Max the Sax ahh boy oh boy
he blew the storm outside to shame
whew it was some wail it was the tops
he made all four seasons in three measures
boy he blew sweet silk
your skin is sweet silk your neck
pulses my tongue draws up
at your chin & there balances
just like Finnegan's great note yes very just
his scaredy wavering high high tin G
how how long did we guess did we tremble
it fell momentous he pulled us down
rockslides of scales maximum piano crash
man oh man how them workingmen roared
& their ladies my lady your eyes roar my God
they change color your face is dim but they do
I swear so soft grey to blue
ooo meet my eyes & then your spine
smooth sensitive oh down down ooo make it be
delicate your lips quiver yes
vibrant your heart is sweet fleshy rhythm yes
bad as all life in these human breaths

THE BEAR

I woke to scuffling dirt and leaves
beyond my tent.
I raised my head an inch or two
and lay in dark, attentive, poised,
until with prickling neck I sensed
a cautious snuffling at my feet,
a soft snort and grunt—
I froze, and lay breathlessly listening
to the breeze, for minutes only
the breeze, and my skin slowly calmed.
Then a curious creeping passion drew me
out of my tent, out of fear,
into the night. The moon shone
brilliantly round in the clear air,
the mountainside gleamed,
the stars variously pulsed.
I gazed in peace, almost forgetting,
when near upon a precipice
against the sky I saw that form,
that lurking silhouette, that creature watching.
It shifted, caught the light—
and let a wail, a cry, a call
resounding over hills—
It struck me through, it called
to me, I felt that dense emotion
and the gravid love of its land,
and knew that it cried not to me
but to the night, the earth, life
—to all at once. Nothing stirred.
My spine seethed. The stars blinked.
And it was gone, had left me
with loud silence and an image,
the looming black flank glistening.
I know were I to pierce that hide
I would undelve intestine, bolus,
bile, blood, paramecia—and yet
the breathing animal body bears more,
which now I crave.
I saw the beast accept the night
and heard the night in it.
That must suffice.
To touch the dark
velveteen nape, to smell
the heavy damp fur,

to hear the footsteps
departing in shadows
remains desire.

I DAPHNE MAY

I'd have my mind the breeze,
My body wood. Fail,
Agility that restricts my
Knowing the moon without thought,
Let me be still free.
I'd have sap my senses,
Fluttering leaves my heart for the air.

JUAN FELIPE HERRERA

MISSION STREET MANIFESTO

for all varrios

Blow out the jiving smoke the plastik mix the huddling straw of the
   dying mind
and rise sisters rise brothers and spill the song and sing the blood that calls
the heart the flesh that has the eyes and gnaws the chains and blow
and break through the fuse the military spell the dreams of foam
make the riff jump the jazz ignite the wheel burn the blade churn rise
and rise sisters rise brothers and spill the song and sing the blood that calls
the ancient drums the mineral fists the rattling bones of gold
on fire the lava flow the infinite stream the razor wave
through the helmet the holy gun the Junta the seething boot
shake it do the shing-a-ling the funky dog of sun and moon
pull out the diamonds from your soul the grip of light the stare of stars
rip the wires invade the air and twist the scales and tear the night
go whirling go singeing go shining go rumbling go rhyming
our handsome jaws of tender truth our shoulders of sweating keys
to crack the locks the vaults of hands the dome of tabernacle lies
and rise sisters rise brothers and spill the song and sing the blood that calls
out swing out the breathing drums the tumbling flutes the hungry strings
and spin a flash deep into the sorrow of the silent skull
the vanquished lips the conquered song the knot in the belly of earth
break out through the fenders the angel dust kiss the methodone rooms
go chanting libre chanting libre go chanting libre go
libre *La Mission* libre *El Salvador* libre *La Mujer*
the will of the worker now the destiny of children libre
blow out the jiving smoke the plastic mix the huddling straw of the
   dying mind
the patrolling gods the corporate saints the plutonium clouds
strike the right the new Right to crucify the right to decay
the triple K the burning cross the territorial rape game
and stop the neutron man the nuclear dream the assassination line
the alienation master the well groomed empire the death suit
and rise and rise libre libre and rise and rise and rise libre
and rise sisters rise brothers and spill the song and sing the blood that calls
blow out the jiving smoke the plastik mix the huddling straw of the
   dying mind
forever
forever
forever.

from PHOTO-POEM OF THE CHICANO
MORATORIUM 1980 / L.A.

Photo 1. Pilgrimage

The march is holy. we are bleeding. the paper crosses unfold
after ten years. stretching out their arms. nailed. with spray
paint. into the breasts of the faithful. followers. they bleed
who we are. we carry the dead body. dragging it on asphalt
America. we raise our candle arms. our fingers are lit. in
celebration. illuminating. the dark dome of sky. over Whittier
Boulevard. below. there are no faces. only one. eye. opening its
lens. it. counts the merchants locking iron veils. silently
secretly. as we approach. their gold is hidden. they have
buried diamond sins in the refrigerators. under the blue
velvet sofas. they are guarding a vault. of uncut ring
fingers. the candles sweat. who tattooed the santo-man on our
forehead? Ruben Salazar. we touch the round wound with saliva
the clot of smoke. a decade of torn skin. trophies. medallions
of skull. spine. and soul. spilled. jammed. on the grass. gone
forever. beneath the moon-gray numbers of L.A.P.D. August 29
1970. running. searching for a piece. of open street. *paraíso
negro.* pleading to the tear-gas virgins. appearing over the
helmet horns of the swat-men. iridescent. we walk. floating
digging deep. passing Evergreen cemetery. passing the long
bone palms shooting green air. stars. as we count the death
stones. burning. white. rectangles. into our eyes. processions
have no gods. we know. they know. the witnesses. on the sidewalks
the thirty-two year old mother with three. children. no
husband. by the fire hydrant. the bakers. the mechanics leaning
on the fence. spinning box wrenches. in space. the grandfather
on the wheelchair saluting us. as we pass. as we chant. as we
scream. as we carry the cross. a park with vendors appears
ahead

Photo 2. Oasis/We Gather/Audience/Wide-Angle

We drink tropical waves. unknown lips of sun &
fragrant oils slip. down our backs. *nos reímos*
camaradas. we gather & we scope the elements
the cop helicopter will never invade our lake
it will never drink our perfume. today we make
this crazy speck of twin-blades blow. away. with
our eyes. la Kathy from East Los. el David &
his chavalo Noel. la Eva rapping with Cesar
el Bobby. Valentin & Francisco. we slap the air
hard. pulsating. opening the rock. around our
bodies. liquid. flesh. pouring. circling. entering
the grass. el saxofón blows hearts & lightning &
Felix sings quarter notes. *chale con el draft*
pulling at his chinese beard. el Aztleca talks
about the cultural center in San Diego. power
plays in the dance group. we pull at the grass
snipping stems. making incense for miniature
altars. who can fill the chasms in the corners
around the shoes? the black net stockings
silhouette cliffs & shifting gravel stains
the shirt-tails. a question mark of buttons
surrounds the waters. flashing against the flat
buildings. we gather. in the light

Photo 3. The Speakers

Fellini said only clowns know the truth. they smile
in torture. never speaking. although their sound
explodes and destroys. children appreciate them. naturally
children are their teachers. a good clown always
learns from the rhythms and the voiceless somersault
of a child. children are the first to experience disorder
joyfully. they attack madness with their round bellies.
pushing into its darkness. plucking its hairs. it tickles
them. they dream of being slayers of the monster. they
gather. they stand on a mound. imagining they can speak
to it. so. they mumble. swaying their wooden swords

Photo 6. Night/Aftermath/The Mime at Figueroa St./Tri-X

for Adrian Vargas

The mime moves. lightly. he teaches us political ballet
step. by step. his eyes have bodies. that stretch. far
into the air. of Latin America. tiller-woman. tiller-
man. beneath the *patrón*. the military. *La Junta*
fevers in plantations. deliriums. in Haciendas. still
El Salvador. light bodies. explode in cathedrals
the yearning chests multiply. into honeycomb spilled
muscles. flayed. floating. caught in the bamboo
gyrations of his eyes. feather-weight tendons. shutter
as he snaps the head left. staring into the room
of people on chairs. lined up. against the off-white
wall stamped with photo 1. the march. photo 2. a woman
speaking. photo 3. leaders at the microphone. photo 4.
undercover agents. photo 5. people fleeing. cut. dying
in 1970. he stares. over the bannister. past our
shoulders. past. the gallery wall. seeing us. rumble
murmur. rumble. scream. pushing. we sweat. smoking
jive. with cans of alcohol. wet offerings. to unknown
deities. seeing the moist walls behind us. open
the single eye. pointing steady. shooting. across the
horizon moon swaying its tattooed flesh through
the city. compounds of swollen curtains. an apartment
with a hallway altar. a boy passes by the crucifix
bronze. body of Christ. guarding a bouquet of plastic
day-glow roses. a blue candle vase. tapping light
rhythms on the ceiling. whispering lips of smoke
at the. end. an opaque window. shut. closing out
the night of violent winds and soft movements.

KATHARINE HARER

SOQUEL

for Patrice Vecchione

It's lovely to wake up in a house
where women walk naked

She is cream   too soft

the frame of the doorway
dissolves for her

and in the hanging mirror   waterlike
thistle of sleep in our mouths

we are Matisse's girls

She has long breasts
she carries the collected dark
of sleep

the scar of a small white lake
across her thigh

We braid the house   crunch toast
open streams of water

walk more softly than light

Look how the mirror in the just
perceptible air

holds us
and lets us pass

THE PALM MOTEL

for T.G.

There's nothing desolate about the dogs
who hang their tongues on the night

or the trucks that lower their heavy weight
into our hands

There's a country in the imagination
with trees of soft fruit
there are people waiting for us
we've never seen

we enter through the silences of roadside cafes
the flat talk of fish and weather

Strangers come to us in early morning
without their clothes

we take them into our beds
and make love with them

under the unforgettable trees

ROGER APLON

TRAILING THE ARMY

There are armies
crossing Nebraska.
Armies that fatten on leftover cows
armies so silent and sure
they lumber over the day
unmindful of sweat
forgetting rivers
crossed and recrossed.
I am trailing the army
gouging huge holes in their water bags
clipping the sharp eyes of their bayonets
exhausting their mothers with stories
of past atrocities.
Someone has to follow.
Someone must nip at the wide black haunch.
They are well organized and have learned
the rewards of cutting
everything down.
Everything that grows on its own
is suspect.
No one has survived the wave on wave
of their perfect form.
Even the frogs
fall game.
The nights are filled with their music;
They mimic the chords and pipes of human throats.
In Kansas City there are people
already overcome.
In St. Louis there are people of knowledge
catching planes.
In Detroit
no one has even begun to care.

IF YOUR SKIN

for R

If your skin were fine sand
I'd burrow
to the bone
planting apples for the morning

If your skin were slate
I'd chisel leaves
and branches
bowed with yellow blossoms

If your skin were moss
I'd drift in the tendrils
sleep between your ribs
with the drowsy snails

If your skin were oil of cobalt blue
I'd scribble fingers
with long strokes
up and down the breathing of your spine

If your skin were field grass
I'd rake the cuttings gently
sucking down
the faint odor of rain

If your skin were rivers
I'd bob for crayfish in the pools
rescue quail and white peacocks
from the flooded banks

If your skin were air
I'd conjure bats to glide
mercilessly
through the waves of tiny flying eyes

If your skin were ice
I'd wrap you in the womb of a wolf
stroking her belly
with oil of mulberry and eucalyptus

If your skin
under my hands

almost iridescent
in this dark room
reached warming

your sealed, secret, supple
skin...

JULIA VINOGRAD

THE CONCRETE ANNUNCIATION

I have seen the street lights wearing haloes after a rain;
they were not misplaced.
I have seen the stopsigns wearing bright barbaric crowns,
cruel and imperial as some ancient Assyrian tyrant.
I have seen the crowd of worshippers
going slowly and reverently after a parking space.
I have seen the clothes of custom fall from tongues in a bar
and feelings dance naked as a child
being fed to the equally naked flames.
I have seen drunks on the cold stone altar of a back alley
sacrificed to the sharp knife of dawn.
I have seen sex made into blasphemy,
a splendid insult unto heaven,
rare and impossible as the unicorn,
dangerous as the dragon
and all for whatever the going price can get away with.
I have seen waitresses branded with their smiles.
I have seen the shadow beast of work nipping at many heels,
hurry and worry and money, it breathes.
I have seen landlords lording it over their rooms,
each a crystal in a chandelier
and the tenant as the light within is also owned.
I tell you I have seen the city possessed by a passionate god,
caught unprepared and panting between her cement sheets
and all her crumbling crayon cosmetics.

LONESOME

Everyone lives in lonesome these days,
furnished room lonesome, split-level lonesome.
Lonesome's a big dark wind blowing behind the eyes,
blowing poems and lovers and crumpled newspapers away,
all blown into lonesome, all blown down into lonesome.

Lonesome's much longer than time,
big snake lonesome eats clocks whole,
coils around days and squeezes,
lonesome venom fevers nights,
lonesome snakebites where the stars bleed thru.
Big old lonesome with the world inside
where everyone lives, not looking, not looking,
scared to see lonesome so don't see anything,
scared to feel lonesome so don't feel anything
and lonesome keeps growing and blowing away.
Everyone lives in lonesome these days.

 ## BATTLE CALL

Send me your young awkward men
with their beautiful guns
for I am death
and I am never satisfied.
Send me a pile of lovers
to polish my virgin bones.
Send me the last great war
again
to bark at my feet and show its fangs
each decorated with ribbons of extreme valor,
for I need another poodle to take me out on walks
where all the places young men used to stand
will whistle at my shadow.
Send me your women's curses,
how can they compete
with my brand new toys
dangerous as a drunken dare
and as hard to refuse.
Send me fresh blood
to make my lips shine.
For I am death and won't be seen
until my face looks right.
For I am death and won't go out alone.
Come with me, take me dancing.
I am death
and I've been so lonely for you,
baby.

JACK HIRSCHMAN

THE PORTRAIT

You were always water to me,
this vessel, this boat
of a body full of
syllables—from you who
accidentally in the sense
of chance, in the French
sense of *hasárd*, gave
me your life to care for,
a life I care for,
fashion from its immense stillness
this noise of propaganda,
this madness but clear sailing
of thirst for your repose:

a love in many places
forming a chin,
many lenses forming a pair
of eyes,
many forms of hair forming
a form of hair,
whose silence makes others speak,
who exist outside of my
hearing you—

    I am sick of hearing a world
call you shit
call you bad
call you weird
call you the devil
call you god.

    I live with you eternally;
when I see face inside
my face, it is yours,
when I smash the barriers
of usury and vice,
of all the mechanisms of
capital and the inventions

of steel used to defend them,
when I fill with comrades
and streets, wires and volts
of religious creeds,
it is you who see me through
the struggle to feel
your form again,

face, communist face,
that never will I sell
to the machinery of woe,
face I will go to my grave with,
simple face, face of nature,
style of a century artificed
and complex,
whose journey *is* to face
the face of pure
confrontation within,
to be destroyed into poem
again and again by it,
to be reborn with the millions
of other red faces,
face of my handsweat,
face I defend against
the violence of time
of history kissed
in prisons of thighs,
in prosodies of wires of diplomacies,
face which multiplies
from the one,
from the bipolar forms
of bridgings and abdominal cries,
face of chance
I have rendered
eternally revolutionary,
turning from everything
backward, revisionist,
merely historical,
to keep me,
no matter how
many changes

    of music, of
    records,
    of lovers,
    of streetcars,

of conversions to
religions
of whirligig lies,

read with you
as a breath
for which there is
no breathing but everything
fills with lung,
no movement but everything
is in motion,

and what it names
is the stillness,
the silence;
from which will emerge
the minutiae and grandiosity
of these dialects
of a tribe
it purifies

with every thought
of its resolution
and its revolution
as the word

WHEN SHE IS TYPSY

I am the child of people
who love to work in order to love
in order to sing in order
to sleep in the broken glass of the moon
till the sun comes up
and it's time to serve the light.
There is no right wing on
this red winging bird,
two left wings make us awkward
at times,
two pieces of wire hold this
dumdum poem together,
that is, hold it down in the gutter,
hold it where the butter still
    can be felt,
where the taste inside warm
bread
is very close to what a woman
is inside,
and wine is natural as
blood between men of honor.

JERRY RATCH

from PUPPET X

IV

I'm not a practising angel,
ladies & gentlemen

Got these penny wings
out of boredom

I need to know
that black & grey place
inside an angel
where you bow your head,

when a puppet
forgets himself,

when a man learns
how small deer laugh

   —that we live
     singing about lettuce—
     blue lettuce on Thursday...

     (when they turn over a card
     & hand you a rule)

     "a bunny may weep
     a bunny may sleep

     & a big bunny
     may pray
     once in awhile..."

For I must spend time with them

& we will have our hours
ready

V

It's true

When a man goes mad
ropes come down from the clouds

He cannot be sure of anything
Anything

The way's uncharmed
He thinks someone else's strange thoughts

& it all seems a simple trick
Like someone standing all night
on the back doorstep

—The Sea of White Time

—The wet sky
(which, said the pheasant,
does exist)

    "Sleep will tell you
    a pretty green story"
    O heart
        If you return...

Or you're stuck in the traffic
& giant butterflies
light on the fenders
& stagger inside
your windows
(& kiss the ones that live)
in that medieval
way

The hopelessly married
in their cars

The nondescript of
every description
The old & apologetic

—They're all dead, mind you

Their names departing
from them & their children alike

& the butterflies don't
find too much delight
in all the cold
familiar faces

The necessity of rules
& jewels
& matters of the chest...

They would have lived simply,
given birth,
& fallen back into the earth—

If it had not been for the horror
of the passage...

& at the same time
the carrots are
kicking them in the ass

saying
Have a good
time,
kids

X

Still
I don't know

One minute you're
squeezing the brains out of
goldfish, the next
you're running the
show

After awhile
it's hard to raise an eyebrow over
anything

—the sound of
lightly falling souls

—your crotch cold & dreaming:

        pneumonia   oldmonia
        6 is half a dozen

Is the way you
would say it
I suppose...

It shouldn't
have to be
that way

        —raised to forget quickly
        —smiling around

        —used to being artificial

The dead dislike themselves
The living
are in pain

What hopelessness, misery,
despair
One thinks of washing his hands
One doesn't care...

We know   the rules   we know

—the road to Standard City

ROBERT ANBIAN

THE DYING MAN'S SHAME

I'm a raw meat inhabits these walls
where they've slung huge blades
—stonehandled broadswords, fishlike rapiers,
broadaxes!—through the windows,
under doors, come waving out of the drains!
Where in the popping skin of night
I grunt, swell and salivate,
under the rock of these others
beneath the spotlight of the moon.

The killer sat in these chairs,
walked about the room, crawled the length of the hall,
came, left, remained, lay in this dirty bed.
A lithe being come sweeping after us in our own steps—
                                        yours and mine,
together!—like our fathers, our lost lovers, our
                                        drunken drivers
hurled from behind, speechless, thrilled
back of slowmotion lids, between bad lips.

Once we were making love in the light of the day
—you remember!—and we expired on a land mine,
under an atom bomb, beneath the weight
of a coup dressed-up in rags.
They guillotined us inch by inch
on a pedestal before a mad mob.
It was the bed into which we settled
chewing our ears in the light of my mother's lamp,
down in your father's cellar, other siblings boiling
in the vines in the window lattice.

Then the bricks like convicts sweated into the room
which leaned upon my face of a butcher's son, and you,
dancing cruelly as a fascist,
deep in the earth's ear
in the gorge of a cry.

I want to die out of doors with the animals!

I want to die wrapped in a forest
not in these stinking sheets! Won't you—if you are
                              a comrade!—abandon me
to the rock shore
of an inky pond, in the cup of the hills
where the eyes of beasts dart about
like tadpoles in a breathing sea.
Listen! I don't want to die in these sheets, in this red
                    room, on your conspiratorial bosom.
I want to die in the open air, with the beasts, in
                         a slow dusk, in a fragile century.

OLD WOMAN

I came across her today, that old woman
who longed after my grandpa
and never forgot his treachery or his teeth.
The old woman who gave her tits away.
The old woman who bore loving bastard sons
and saw them explode on a yellow field.
The old woman who housed a daughter
in her ribs, wept over her and washed her toes
and saw her give birth to a green stone.
The old shopping-bag woman who planted flowers,
cut them, and sold them for pennies.
The old woman who couldn't eat pennies.
The old woman who died
and sits up in her coffin refusing to lie down.
Her old hands sawing in the air, her eye sockets wet,
her charred lips working over bald gums, she says,
"Haven't you any love left
for this old woman?"

OCEANOLOGY

I'd loved and lost you so often
the sands were turning to molten
glass, and the sea to marble
and the fish alas! were teeming
into my heart's little inlet.
It's true they were a school taught me
narrow bones. I gave up,
went away, a real sea voyage, lost my hair, my rights,
my citizenship. Well enough, I said to no one at all,
I didn't need any of that. On the day everyone's past jumped
ship for a sentimental whore in a port
with a name like a famous knife, I said
ditto by me. So long! I yelled,
waving my blue trousers, don't take
any bad shots! And when the horizon
smoked its candle-wick
in the opened window,
I said okay. Alright. I'll steer by the sound
of the planets, rushing in arithmetical currents
of a Milky Way burning in my scalp.
Out of liquor in time and below decks, I discovered
I'd used up my last surmise of consort. My ship then
was my despair,
rotted and rolling in the swells,
turning and twirling and twisting and going down
in a dead spot of water, my eternal city
wizening in an abandoned mirror. Was the silence
made me tremble. At the precise instant
of the disappearance of my three masts,
which made three tiny whirlpools
on the glazed surface of an unrealized Southern Ocean

I found you,
ensconced in a cool rock
midst the singular Atlantis
where souls go who have committed
a grave mistake. A glistening snail had curled itself
in your ear, and the oceanidic music of your regret
threw its anemones—yellow, pink, amber—onto
    the currents
of these green veritable waters. Surrounded

by delicately chested sea horses, your olive
flesh full of the sea, you saw
I did not weep, but sucked on your toes while above us
continents burned, and children,
on the red beaches, skipped gaily through mineral hoops.

PAUL MARIAH

GRAVEL

We remember well
We spent
The day watching the

Gravel King, blue
Over
Alls. He had no one

Else to talk to so
He'd
Pick up a handful

Of small grey rocks &
Talk
To them very serious

Ly, indeed! Then he'd
Put
Them singly in his mouth

So he'd hear the answers
Sharp,
Clarity against his red tongue.

He knew the whole prison
Yard
By the feel of his tongue

Against each grey rock.

THE FIGA

I want you to know
how it feels
to have a fist
the size of a poem
up your ass.

Get the vaseline.
This is one finger
and if I angle right
I can get past the knuckle.
Hold still.
This is two fingers
introduce rhythm
fingermovements
allow the play to continue
This is three fingers
Keep the rhythm steady
never stop the movement
I want you to feel the size of
This is four fingers
Cupped and the play continues
and I am not going to stop
Lift the left leg higher
This is my thumb
and the movement is steady
the fingers move into
you are closing around my wrist.

Now how does it feel
to have a poem
shoved up your ass
the size of a fist?

Now, I am going to uncup
my palm and make
a scratch on the inside.

This was the scene
and I had to get out of bed
to write it
so you would know
the size of it
and now we can go on...

A HERD SONG : AN ELEPHANT MINUET

A herd of elephants is dancing on my roof.
They have come with long trunks and thick ears,
With tarbuckets and gravel to repair
Winter's cold tracks. They wear asbestos
Smiles all over their faces. They won't wash off.

The siding they give one another in play.
A heard-song, an elephant minuet on my roof.
The wood nymphs in construction boots skate
Across the roof on brooms, on ladders.
They have come to tarpaper the ground

Of my sky, they have come to tarpaper heaven,
With their trucks, long rods, confectioner's
Sugar sacks to collect the last cold of winter
And bury it under the roll of hot asbestos...
It won't wash off. There's no ecology there.

But the rumblings of the hours, all the galls
Are clinking like at a wake or an earthquake.
A heard-song, an elephant minuet on my roof.
They communicate with ropes and buckets of tar.
They attempt to sing, the whole herd, with shovels.

Their divining rods are forty feet long but
They cannot sing with their feet stuck. Ox
Ygen tanks & fire coagulate the morning sun.
Smiles all over their faces. They won't wash off.
A herd of elephants is dancing on my roof.

KAREN BRODINE

THERE IS A REFUSAL TO BE DROWNED

that floats my breasts up plump
in the tub   that wants the fat moon
to tongue the uncurtained glass
that lets my hands find you and continue
to want   there is a refusal
to be drowned   that buoys me up
from a silent man to tread water
toward you   how many times
have we talked until light   if we shape
poems   discarding a sock   a blouse   a bad
line   a shoe   how long till we live
unnightgowned together speaking
in tongues

WHAT SHE DID IN MY DREAM

The reason the dream keeps coming back is it keeps
being true. The branch keeps springing into my face
because it is the same path. This time I see the woman
has a wide brow and grey eyes. She tells me to walk
up that path and write how it is to be a woman
who has decided to have no children. Dusk evens out
the sharp brambles. As I climb it easily darkens
to full night. I hear the faint joyful voices of children
that run past me down the path. I come to a structure
built of sweetsmelling new wood, climb the ramp,
switch on a light bulb. Seeing how bare and empty it is,
I think, "but this will be a good place to work."

from CENSORSHIP

1. The Words

All my life, the urgency to speak, the pull toward silence.
Embodied in the two sides of the family: like a tree
without a mouth, my Swedish father, bottled up and bursting
out in mean words, or averting his eyes unable to say goodby;
he goes back in the house, he shuts the door, he wants to
feed us berries and fish and things he has grown, he watches
us talk and laugh and our joy is reflected briefly in his
eyes, but he can only watch as if we are a painting, beautiful,
but out of reach. And my mother and grandmother, Jewish,
overflowing with words, loving to talk about people, never
can I rival their stories of people's foibles, to laugh
with but never at, the amazing quirks of neighbors and friends.
Me with one ear tuned to the strungtight wires of my father's
hands as he picks raspberries. We are singing, "I'll take
the high road and you take the low road." He rolls the berries
of the tall bushes into a coffee can, while I eat the berries
from the lower vines. We sing but we don't talk.

Inside the house, in the cool, intimate, wisteria-shaded
kitchen, my mother and grandmother are talking, they have
been talking all afternoon, I hunch under the table,
scratching my name on the bare wood with a stubby pencil.
They are laughing and a chair scrapes and a cup clinks as
my mother pours more coffee. I love the talk of my two
women parents, but I know how often it crosses the border
between relaxation and direction: Karen, help your mother
a little once in awhile, Karen go get me a good head of
lettuce from the garden, so I listen, but I hide under the
table to listen in peace.

As to my own talking, this will take awhile; no one could
rival my grandma, so I must wait until she's out of earshot
to hear myself think. But my mother and me, we talk and we
listen, we go back and forth, and from her I learn the
company of words, the clarity of faces turned together in
interest, focused through speech.

And when I see her words muffled or stopped mid-sentence or
slapped back in her face with derision, or simply not even
begun, I know the first rule of censorship, that it goes
with sadness, with someone wronged, or stopped, the shades
drawn, the expression dropping down into bitterness, so for

years I ask her anxiously out of the blue, "What's the matter?
What's the matter?" And she will never tell me but I know.

The first rule of censorship is a woman cramped in the grid of
economy and house, family and duty, powerless, held in, stopped
short. And the second rule is that in a hundred small ways, she
resists and then all at once when I am eighteen, she bursts out
to live alone, to say whatever she wants. So I learn to
follow her way and speak out too.

GIRLFRIENDS

well **she said,**
my hairdresser's gay
and all that, but
two women: I just can't
understand it.

1.

the brain begins
as shadow
and grows
into a wing.

Shelley,
you thought
you could fly out that window,
long hair streaming after—
I held on
like furniture
determined
as an owl.

in a scribble
my face twisted red
my mouth roared
in an O
my hands

flared
into feathers.

2.

they stole the harp
snapped each string
the harpist
couldn't weep
look, her fingers
are quills
see, her wrists
are white down.
when we were young,
we were twins.
I stretched barbwire
taut, you
slipped through,
turned to hold.
we strummed
the woods,
sapling,
rode the creek
on the rafts
of our bodies—
remember?
how we traded
blouses
how your mother
was angry
at us so much
together

3.

my wrists
now economical,
my knees no longer
pale burglars in
breathless hose.

I battle daily
a crazy old woman
feed her pellets
of soft bread, rolled
in my palms.

yes, I tell her, yes,
old bird, old scissor,
all that you suspect
is true. my lover, she

and I, we live in a tub,
we pop small stones, salty
into our mouths.
wet, they flame
blue and red,
shining with mica.
now chew on that!

quelled, she
vanishes, but
she'll be back
haze before rain
feathers confusing
the rug, a pillow
exploding

THE WOLVES WERE SILVER

the wolves were the silver flecked grey of salmon
and thin bellied   they slipped among us barely brushing
our thick clothes   the sheep we kept were so white against
the snow   they could only be discovered by their shadows
we knew they were there in need of protection   an old
woman among us said the snow would likely deepen and
the bridge collapse underneath the weight   some people
had frozen and we took these dead ones in our arms and
tossed them up into the air   they landed under the bare
trees and the wolves minnowed toward them, belly-flat
to the snow   we drew into a close safe pack   we had
to keep touching

DAVID MELNICK

THE REGULARS

my royal tables
taste
      of.
breathe
    cannot weep.   clocks.

know the slowest

clocks
  in the universe. ocean
                  know the parts of
you   're the least conscious of, grace you cannot observe

close my eyes in every room
  to yr absence

              moon
                truth, desolation or horse.

how can we shun it?
sits and weeps
            ashes words rocks mice

structure
its variations and delight

        weary days, fear of natures law

coral
   &
   gold

     tear the branches
three weeks of space, three weeks of space & labor

                The German

Why do we mouth?
what word, what day,

                    appetite,
      neighbor.
          least of all 'your family'
                         a curve of silk
                         hangs in the palace window
your torso.   your thigh.

Why, now, at the end of his life, a new dimension?
all those rites, her intense delight.

I was walking. you were.
the careful blade between
truth
       canyons
&
   hysterical brainings.

this was not easy, this wasting, crowding, a row of chambers,
               the ring on the floor, the flight.

Where was the night I

           lavas, bombs, pumice

                         over April or Daisy and

                         sea blue bruise a
                                       fine
corpus in the sexual palace angel alienate
                         angel
                         alienate from inches & tongues

      when you look for matter you can only begin
      after 'life' has turned it self
      out & framed an area of action apart and
      strange.
      to recapture.

(easy & familiar.)

      the plastic telephone, and the plastic
      table
                         readiness to flatter if

by the skin that speaks the soft hello.

FRANCES MAYES

COUSIN

Downstairs our fathers
in their dark suits
divided the Sunday paper
The table was cleared
its wax grapes back in place
From the porch Willie
shook out the linen cloth
and looked down Lee Street
where it was summer
or winter or fall

We were sent upstairs with books
to rest in grandmother's bed
Our best dresses fell
in soft heaps of blue and green
In Hazel's old room
the mothers murmured of wallpaper
and what a shame it was....
Across the hall, afternoon
flat and gold, ticked for us
in the vest pocket of our grandfather
bald and breathing deep
his hands locked on his chest

We unhooked our black shoes
from Atlanta, whispering in our slips
In the smothered quiet
her closet opened without a sound
We took out her feather hats
the mauve scarves and the three
foxes with flat stomachs
stitched in silk

We wrapped ourselves in them
staring in the mirror
at the savage little faces
that warmed her
the fur on our shoulders

matted with her scent
of lavender and dust
Not daring to open the dull rose
nailpolish, we stole dimes from the box
she'd collected for cancer
Ruthless and plundering
we laughed behind her black veils
stuffing our bosoms full of stockings

At the first sound
we darted to the high bed
where we sank like snow angels
into the deep coverlet
Above us was the swoop of lace
our grandmother crocheted
the handspans linked like white
spider webs or snowflakes cut from paper
Stiff as dolls we lay waiting
for someone to come
halfway up the stairs
and, in case we might be sleeping
softly call our names

ROB GOLDSTEIN

SOMEWHERE

for Laura Feldman

Amy is seated   on a large rock in the middle
of the long island sound. Eric cavorts on the shore.
He is the straw man   scattering pieces of himself
here and there in case he gets lost. Amy   shrieks
her desire to anyone who'll listen. Eric is transfixed.

The beach is dark. Eric lights a piece of straw. The
flame shoots across the sky like a warning. He reaches
for Amy. A scale breaks off. "Your skin is like sequins."
He blushes   at his confession.

"This morning," Amy says, shifting on the rock
for comfort, "I felt the plushness of your belly
and thought of the sweating fur of horses. But then,
most men   remind me of that."

Tonight the moon rises synchronized to the swell
of Hawaiian music. All sigh and wonder how the musicians
have managed it. Amy   her head on Eric's shoulder, dreams
of the races.

II

He lies. "I
look at you. Suck in my breath. My hands tremble. The
color of my feet change. These things distress me." He
is not convincing.

Amy splashes the water listlessly.

An evening star spreads its points across the sky. Orange
spray across the peak of Diamond head. Amy rocks her head
from side to side. Beach shells and seaweed. The single foot
print of a transient. "I think I'll go now," she says
with a flip of her fin.

PROCREATION

Your gums tease
the length
of his cock.

A slick benefit of old age.

Future lover,
which flickering body
on the screen brings
you arousal?

and you old man.

How adroitly you
nip him
in the bud.

MICHAEL PALMER

LEFT UNFINISHED SIXTEEN TIMES

I is the director of three letters and the dead director.

And I is the reader's "not yet" within the letter.

I includes the one incapable of mentioning death in the event, or else the director or else the dead letter.

(This could be said not to be written.)

I is enclosed by the question where it's read as a letter.

I might pretend to be a reading in the letter, its circuit diagram or "music hall full of fun" or weighing of symptoms and costs.

I refers to the pause or loss, the decision that a window will remain closed the better to watch.

I thought it would be nice to make some chemicals, to make some lexical adventures to enlarge the space, then reside forever in the silence of the letter.

I is directed by the names of three letters, unnaming the dead director.

And I is the reader's forgotten letter.

Where I is mentioned there is a pause or loss, a papered hall lit at intervals by backward letters.

Where I goes unmentioned there exists an alternate version filled with cups, diagrams, quills and jars.

Perhaps a farm beneath the sea.

This omits, perhaps deliberately, the question of the head and neck, position of the hands, and the rope between her teeth drawn slowly across the floor.

It omits or forgets who they are and who the others are who watch.

Then it forgets the words for this and not-this, for first and for again.

Then imitating I he says, "Forgetfulness must be remembered when you insist 'I cannot remember.' " Who is it will admit to this.

SONG OF THE ROUND MAN

for Sarah when she's older

The round and sad-eyed man puffed cigars as if
he were alive. Gillyflowers
to the left of the apple, purple bells to the right

and a grass-covered hill behind.
I am sad today said the sad-eyed man
for I have locked my head in a Japanese box

and lost the key.
I am sad today he told me
for there are gillyflowers by the apple

and purple bells I cannot see.
Will you look at them for me
he asked, and tell me what you find?

I cannot I replied
for my eyes have grown sugary and dim
from reading too long by candlelight.

Tell me what you've read then
said the round and sad-eyed man.
I cannot I replied

for my memory has grown tired and dim
from looking at things that can't be seen
by any kind of light

and I've locked my head in a Japanese box
and thrown away the key.
Then I am you and you are me

said the sad-eyed man as if alive.
I'll write you in where I should be
between the gillyflowers and the purple bells

and the apple and the hill
and we'll puff cigars from noon till night
as if we were alive.

NANCY LAMBERT

FINAL EXAM

part one. multiple choice
san salvador beirut moscow athens new
york lisbon hanoi tel aviv dublin kingston
havana miami peking bombay seoul teheran
pick a place
any place
make one
up
be
creative. in the year 1871 1492 197d3
which one of the above was liberated
or purged of children in order to
save them. be specifi
cally in what year of your lord pick a
lord
any lord
make one
up
be
creative, what offense by what troop of
advisors or what jet flew due west or
east for what summit. precise
ly at noon when that generalrahjahking sword
in hand held what banner what
freedom what progress. concise
ly in gutters wedged bodies slit pulp
and their heartmeat still pulsing on chests
black or brownbrown or yellowredpaisley red
checkered stripeslashed wide with
what shade of blood. elo
quently make poem
make a good one
three
metaphors. in 38532 016 1sevnteen B c what sound
did scream freedom freedom FREEDOM I
can't hear you make what BOMB
burst the gunbolt the snapping of
bones. in wwTWO warsaw who saw the song
the penned Jew sang. none of the

above. which war fill in the blank and they
take up their OWN ARMS NOW keep
in mind the gun articulate unforgotten
the march for NOWAR for equalityeco
logyPEACE censored met/ignored by
violence the
leftRight an
essay on
poignance. the span of one life span
of HIStory ape to pure mind ape to
insect to houseplant to dragonURTH sifting
your bones through the meadows your
fruit rolling flesh on tongues of
rock.
in what year was hunger or gout
and the gorging of flesh into fats. in
what year will smile fashion prayer re
distribute all WEALTH and with eyes sunken
gauntcheeked we took up arms in the
streets for example: you kept your gun
in a box on top of the closet. I
held it to my head. I
looked at myself in the mirror
holding the gun to my head. my hands
shook. I sweated. the gun
slid from slick hand my throat parched so
easy to die so   easy to
di   SO EASY TO DIE   so   dieeeeeeee   ʎsɐǝ os
    easy to die   so   so   easy to dieso easy to   easyto
die so   ɐsʎ   die
    eeeee   ʎsɐǝ dieeeee ɐ easy to di todi   so die die die
    easy   to   os   so

    so easy to die   so easy to dieesoeasy   easy
    SO EASY TO DIE   əipoɹʎsɐǝ   SO EASY TO DIE
to die. specifical
ly what year 10,000 years from now humanity   dieeeeeee
moves through an ape to what creature.
what savage still drools at the mouth
of caves pekingNEANDERTHAL. Cromagnon. one
of the above. the next solar eclipse then
30,000 years will the a. flies b. worms.
c. mosquitos be noted for what specific
accomplishments in the sciences and
Artz. precise
ly g one six what bone of penned human unites
with soilseashit to food tilled or sown

by what insect appendage ponders
choose one ETERNITY. give at least four good
quotes to SUBSTANtiate convincin
ly. spelling
counts.
watch your
margin
s.s
s.

part two. fill in the blank
IN THE YEAR BLANK HUMAN BEINGS praise the
lord evolved finally to a new form. a new
blank of hands without fingers webbed
fingers12 fingers on no hand or blank
or two blank or no legs no mouth breath
just pure mind or 0 mind at all lumped in
blank lumps and slithers down the roadswam the
rivers to no road no river just sea
or air no air when insects through
air soup glow blank air uranium scorched
parched by the redwhiteblue sun shrunk or
swelling or heaving about. why
when one eight ninefour when
blank went stark mad on the subway.
the birth weight of infants stuffed blank into
sewers on the streets of Bombay? in one
or two sentences give a complete history
of all the peoples who died by
genocide. use
examples. for
example when we make love let's
make love let's not come
as a protest. when we don't let's
not make love let's fuck keep
on coming and coming as a
protest.

part three. personal essay
in what year were the words murderterror
hatredHorrorpain inscribed on the skulls
of what peoples. a one sentence argument
for the existence of God. a one sentence argument
for the existence of evil citing relevant
nightmares from your own blank
experience. refer

to question one. in when last year23 or next
year 1954nl day after tomorrow was
this year today will it can't be my
god oh my god
damn you leave me alone goAWAY please
if only death would pass me by. if only
a gift like some savior some angel some
ship from the stars. I'm waiting still
please take us sheep flocked cruel
temperment back again to start anew who
said the above. in response to what
question. finally. final
ly write a short essay on silence and
screaming and
sharing and solitude. on sex bake
a cake. all's for
given come Ho
mmmmm

ALICE WALKER

IN UGANDA AN EARLY KING

In Uganda an early king chose
his wives
from among the straight and lithe
who natural as birds of paradise
and the wild poinsettias
grow

(Did you ever see Uganda women? Dainty
are their fingers
genteel their footsteps on the sand)
and he brought them behind
the palace to a place constructed
like a farmer's fattening pen
with slats raised off the ground
and nothing for
an escapable door
he force-fed them bran and milk
until the milk ran down their
chins
off the bulging mounds that filled
their skins

their eyes quite disappeared
they grew too fat to stand
but slithered to the hole
that poured their dinner
enormous seals

Because? *He liked fat wives*
they showed him prosperous!
and if they up and burst
or tore their straining skins
across the splintered floor,
why, like balloons,
he bought some more.

JOHN MUELLER

from BUDADA

BUDDHA...BUDDHA

BUDA...BUDA

BUDADA...BUDADA

BUDAWHEN!

Prisoners Of History!   Time's Proletariat!!   Turn Back!!!
BUDADA HAS COME!!
NOTHING Is Ever The Same!!   NOTHING Matters!!

Awake you Sailors of the Void!
Workers of this Swirl...Unite!
ALL POWER TO THE PARADOX!!

Budada is swell!   Budada is swollen!
Budada is the bubble of the Universe!
Budada is the way you do what you find yourself doing!!
The Man The Artist The Failure Is Budada!

Budada is the weight of air at any altitude
It is the unit of things real
It is light and film, stage and player
Budada is able to see itself seeing!

Budada is the Base Solution
Budada is the Indissoluble Field
Budada is moderation in EVERYTHING, the Magic Chance,
Epiphany of Names, Toxic Constellations, the Nameless Dread,
the making,
the desire for making.

.   .   .

BUDADA IS NO PROBLEM!!!

Budada Dances Budada is The Dance!
Budada dances nasty!   Honky Tonk Budada!   Slide By
Budada!   Eyes Hot For Budada!   Budada Slick!

YOU CAN DREAM ON BUDADA!
YOU CAN CREAM ON BUDADA!

Budada is...In The Midst Of It All...A Kiss!
BUDADA IS LOVE!   BUDADA COMES!
is Many Colored Fall Guise Budada!

SEX ELECTRO*MAGNETIC BUDADA! REAL PROGRESS BUDADA!

Budada of desperate leaps!
Budada of infinite swiftness and caution!
Budada of the rapids, the big rocks blocking
the Way, Budada for catching the wind.

Budada divides bare fact and certain reality!
Budada wakes up! Budada is reminder,
is remainder, precipitate of childhood!

Power of Will!!   Power of Knowledge!!   Power of Action!!
Budada Is!!!   Unmanifest ground,
Nothing behind every Something, the Beginning!!

BUDADA IS NOT EVERYTHING!

Meticulous Budada!!   Subjective Budada!!

Budada is yr Onlyness, Keeper of the Mask!
Budada is beyond the flowers,
Egg in a hall of mirrors!!

Budada is meta*values!   The arc between Sense
and Nonsense!   Pendulum Budada!   Budada being Where
and What it Sees!   The relative railroad!
The station! The stop and the knowledge:
ETERNAL VIVACITY!!

Happy Chemistry Budada!   Budada Molecule!   DNA Budada!
Budada of Sub*Atomics!   Budada of Electron Wavicles!
Siamese Staircase Budada!   Budada of the Unseen Accident!
BUDADA BOMBARDMENT!!

BUDADA ALERT!!   GO TO YOUR STATIONS!!!
PUT THE LEAD OUT FRONT!!!

Prepare for Budada Apocalypse!!   Be watchful!!
Budada is the Order we do not yet understand!!
Be the muscular fish with the eyes
of the eagle!   Budada is just below the surface!

BUDADA IS GREATER THAN COCA*COLA!!!

NETI NETI BUDADA!!!

Budada the Funanimal Whirled big with Energy!
Open Door Budada!   Window Budada!
PERFECT REFLECTION BUDADA!!

.   .   .

Each moment dies!   Budada watches!
At the exact moment of death,
BUDADA COMES ALIVE!!

BUDADA DELIVERS!!!   BUDADA DELIVERS!!!

Budada is yr Personal Constellation!
Budada Power of Astonishment!
Budada songs of pure delight!
Budada, rediscovered, dances for the Audience of Earth!

BUDADA WILL PREVAIL!!   BUDADA WILL APPEAR,
Erection and Tumescence in the Universal Field!
Ripple Disappear Budada!

Budada is the succession of MAKERS!
Budada the Disconcerted Lens
before which images fly by!   Budada the Sequence
the Conflict the Binocular Arrest!

Keyhole Budada!!   Odds And Ends Budada!!

Budada catches the favorable wind!   Gale Force
Liberation Budada!   Your Mother In Hell
And Once Around the Horn Budada!

Seize the world!   Hold it at arms length!   Budada Repulsion

and Attraction!   Wisdom of billiard balls Budada!
Budada happens between bodies!

The Seven Spiral Stages are Budada!   Dogon Budada!
Budada is the Double Truth at three levels,
The Three Truths identified as One!!

BUDADA WILL SURVIVE AMERICA!!!
BUDADA WILL SURVIVE AMERICA!!!

BUDADA GETS AWAY WITH LIFE!!   BUDADA FELONY!
BUDADA STEALS HOME AND TAKES IT EVERYWHERE!!

On-The-Move Budada!   Gypsy Moth Budada!   Rolling Stone Budada!
Streetwise Budada!   Circus Budada!   Tent-Folding
Sunset Pathmaker Budada!   Always Light
On The Luggage Budada!
Sonic Boom Boom Budada Breaks Away!!

.   .   .

Budada will not choose Virtue till wine and poetry
have been exhausted!   Budada wakes up drunk
on the new day and the way the sunlight enters the room!

Budada is the loss and subsequent recovery.
Budada is the moss that comes back green
following the warm rain.   Budada the frail wings
of the long distance butterfly, the salmon returning,
the albatross re-entering his nest,
coyote peaceful in a new den.

Uroboric Budada Comes Back!!
BUDADA COMES BACK!!   ROUND-TRIP BUDADA!!
OPEN-ENDED RETURN BUDADA!!

.   .   .

San Francisco, 1976

MARTIN MATZ

WHEN MAGUEY SPINES BURN THE WIND

WHEN THE DUST OF MEXICO
            COVERS THE INTESTINES OF MY DREAMS
            I SHALL RETURN
WHEN MAGUEY SPINES BURN THE WIND
            AND THE SKULLS OF DOGS
            PIERCE THE DAWN
      I WILL BE THERE
BROKEN BOTTLES AND CROOKED GRAVES
            DISTURB THE ADOBE SKY
            INDIANS DRESSED IN THE HORNS OF ICICLES
      DANCE ON THE ROOTS OF JULY
MEXICO
            THE SMELL OF RANCID GREASE
                  AND SUNLIGHT
            STICKS TO THE ARMPITS
                  OF MY TORTURED SERAPE
            THE STONES OF PALENQUE
            TRANSFIX MY NAVEL
            AND I AM LOST
      IN A LIQUORISH AFTERNOON
            STUCK TO THE SUN'S SIDE
      WHERE BARRELS OF MOSS
            SING
      IN THE RUINS OF ANCIENT DREAMS
THIS IS THE WAY IT WAS
                        IS
                        SHALL ALWAYS BE
            WITH ONE FOOT STUCK IN
            A POOL OF BURNING MIRRORS
            AND THE OTHER
                  SPINNING
                  A FRENZY OF MICROSCOPES
AS CLOCKS RAPE
            THE FROZEN ASH OF RIVERS
      AND TURN HUMMINGBIRDS TO BRASS
            ON A MOUNTAIN COVERED WITH TEETH.

RICHARD SILBERG

from BELMONT '78

III

When they burst from the gate
there came a roar
it was like the rolling of a wave
and they were running free
Affirmed in front
Alydar a few lengths behind
running easily through the first turn

     The day grew suddenly deep
the horses galloping in that wide green field
sound surging
as thousands of people urged them
praying money
     veins and pop eyes
Danny was screaming beside me
and I felt myself lifted out
into a huge crackling bell of energy

     Alydar starting his move along the back stretch
gaining on Affirmed
         gaining
he pulled even coming into the clubhouse turn
and our minds went white

Alive inside the whale
the cruel beast of History
this race created by New York
as surely as Rome made the circuses
winners and the losers
the rich floating
upon the crushed heads of the poor
to build these instruments of glory

Alydar and Affirmed running together
neck in neck
sculpted heads locked
in a pure Alexandrine straining

galloping the last half mile
in a pitiless stone stretch
like the pumping of some giant heart

And Affirmed won
again
by a nose

Straight up
Danny and I
hugging each other
punching each other
        electrified
        out of our lives

And when he rode back into the winner's circle
this frail piqued eighteen year old in pink silks
                with his arms full of flowers
he was magnified on TV
and we screamed with the crowd
in that beating hollow
fused together shrieking in release
        for Stevie Cauthen
winner of the Triple Crown

A.D. WINANS

ONE TOO MANY POETS
ONE TOO MANY POETRY READINGS

you can always find them in the
back room poised for a quick exit
they're the first poets to read and the
first to leave
they always carry their work with them
in loose leaf notebooks
they always have a pretty girl or boy
hanging on their arms
there is always one who claims
he knew ginsberg or kerouac always
one who claims he slept with one or both

they're usually sandwiched in between
a headache or a hangover or two
2 or 3 live with the gods another
2 or 3 claim they are the
Gods

there is always
one who claims to have
indian blood and who is looking
to get laid
2 ex-junkies   4 homosexuals
a half dozen bi-sexuals and
sometimes a drag queen or two
two sad eyed women rubbing their
hands when they would prefer to be
rubbing something else

always a drop out from the
beat days
a mc clure look-a-like with
a wolf pin in his lapel
a hold over from the flower generation
a nervous lady with short hair
a nervous poet with a tic
always one refugee from the

drug set
one with a poem that drops names faster
than a crazed auctioneer

one poet who reviews poetry in
a local poetry journal
one poet who is an editor
one poet who was an editor
one poet who wants to be an editor

one messiah and
one visiting out of town
star

NEELI CHERKOVSKI

JOSHUA

joshua i said why don't you
pull them down
like a house full of chicken bones
and he laughed at me
and i sat with my thin book and i read to him
about birds and armadillos and roaches and
he sighed and yawned and i told him
    why don't you cave in their chests and
    split open their bellies and i said
    joshua i am behind you and he eyed me
                  suspiciously
and laughed and gave me another drink
  and we made it that night
  with some slave women
and were too tired next morning
  to slit anyones belly.

i said lets burn down the walls
and poison the water and desecrate their
              temple
  and he winked at me
and gave me another drink of wine.

1966

THERE IS A JAVELIN

There is a javelin
      hurtling thru space,
            soon it will land

here, with his name in the center. Then I'll begin

the interesting history
      of love and water. I know

how waves cause lovers to embrace, how wind
of the sea enters every orifice.

Now begins
      the process of waiting.

Ominous gestures of 'life before all of this'
          are played-out, smoothly,

The wrist of the planet
      turns, subtly, and great myths

stand aside.

               1983

JUDY GRAHN

THE QUEEN OF WANDS

And I am the Queen of Wands.
Okay.
Here is how the world works:

It is all like nets.
ever golden, evergreen
the fruits fall
into   hands-like-nets
the fish are hauled
into   jaws-like-nets
the insects crawl
into   claws-like-nets

and the thoughts fall
into   minds-like-nets
it is all like nets.

On the other hand
a spider lives in the topmost branches of a pine,
her house a god's eye gleaming among the needles.
On hot days
she pays out her line and
twirls on down
to the surface of the lake or pond
to get a little drink of water
and to wash her face. She's such an
ordinary person.

The trees line the earth, great and small,
dogwood, plane, maple, rubber,
the elegant palm. The scrubby oak. The elm.
We're ordinary persons, too. We have our
long time friends across the distances,
our urgent messages and our differences.

And we have our parties.
We sugar up our petals just to get the probes of bees in us.
Most green ladies love everything the whipping wind can give them.

The avocado tree hung with her long green breasts,
she aches for fingers pulling at her;
the cherry, peach and nut trees bent with swollen balls
long for hands and mouths and claws;
the fig tree with her black jewels tucked between her
hand-shaped emerald leaves, is happily
fondled by the dancing birds, wild and raucous and drunk on
natural fig wine.

almost any summer morning
sun beams fall into my arms like lovers
giving me everything they've got
and they're so hot   oh honey
I take it all

give it to me, baby
is my song

And I am the Queen of Wands.
The people honor me.
I am the torch they hold over their own heads
as they march march like insects
by the billions
into the bloody modern world,
over discarded corpses of their ages past,
always holding me, aloft or in their arms,
a flame in the hand of the statue,
a bundle of coals
in their inflammatory doctrines, calling me
a chalice of fire,
essential light,
the Flama
and the stuff of which their new world will be made.

Sophia (Helen) they call me, enlightenment,
"God's light," wisdom, romance, beauty, being saved,
"Freedom" and the age of reason.
Progress, they call me, industrial revolution,
"People's rule," the future, the age of
electronics, of Aquarius, of the common man and woman,
evolution
solar energy and self-reliance. Sexual self-expression.
Atomic fission, they call me, physics, relativity,
the laser computations in an endless sky of mind,
"science," they call me and also emotion, the aura of
telepathy and social responsibility, they call me

consciousness, "health," and love
they call me, bloom of Helen.
Blush upon her face, and grace.

And here I am a simple golden shower.
and here I am only a spider
webbing their minds
with pictures, words, impulses
feelings translated into moral imperatives
and rules for living, like leaves
upon a tree, spread to catch the sun's attention.

They (the billions of people)
dance like Fairies on my smallest
twiggiest branches
whistling in each other's ears,
collecting and dispersing
seeds, wearing gold and
pretty clothing, worrying and not
really noticing all the other worlds
around them
how the sun center of my eye sews them
how the silver dream filaments direct them,
how their own thoughts connect them, how
the baton smacks their knees to make them
move their feet, that baton
at the end of the claw
of the Queen of Wands

And I am the tree
with candles
in its fingers
the tree with lights
Menorah
Yule-flame
tree of life

the tree-shaped
candle-holder
on the mantle
on the altar
on the flag of being.

And I am the Queen of Wands
who never went away
where would I go?

the flame is central
to any civilization
any household

any bag of bones. Any motley mote
you've got, of
little mustard seed can grow
into a yellow spicy flame
as you must know.

The sun is a weaver
and the rock earth her instrument.
Slender-fingered threads of light
and heat, dance like birds
shuttling.
Winds and the rain,
seeds and feet and feathers
knit the knot
making the great coat,
the coat of all colors.

The coat of all colors;
over the whole earth, a caught fire
of living logs, brown and red,
tan and white, black and yellow
bobbing like a forest;
each a magic stick with
green flame at its tip

a green web
my leaves, my green filaments
like fingers spread
to catch the sun's attention, spread
to catch the sun like thread,
like sexual feelings, like
the gleam from an eye, or an idea.

and I am the Queen of Wands
I am who stands
who always will
and I am who remembers
the connections woven, little eggs
along the message line.

I remember giving dinosaurs
to the tall unfolded ferns to entertain them.

and immortality to the cockroach.
I remember the birthday of the first
flower, and the death of so many furry
animals and kinds of people, and a star
that fell. I remember a continent
of green
green wands of grass
burning into the knees of
buffalo queens, a landlocked
ocean of fire. Replaced by the
picket fence. Almost equally complex.
Sky scrapers like spikes.
But that's another song.
And I am the Queen of Wands
who burns, who glows, who webs
the message strands,
who stands, who always will.

"LOVE, YOU WICKED DOG"

Love, you wicked dog
so handsome to look at,
so awkward close up
& so unfaithful to good sense.
Whoever feeds you attention
gets you, like it or not. And
all your bad habits come with
you like a pack of fleas.
Wherever I turn for peace of mind
there is the Love dog scratching
at the door of my lonesomeness,
beating her tail against the leg
of my heart
& panting all night with red breath
in my dreams.
Love dog! Get in or out
of the house of my life, stop chewing
on my belongings, the papers &
shoes of my independence.

JACK MARSHALL

FOR SILENCE

In the era of maximum darkness when Light, the Angel
    that was to show Himself, didn't;
In the era when the shrill Kabuki cry shot upward
    from a voice of sand burned to glass, a crystal butterfly
    whose wing-dust had been blown off;
In the era when Language spread her papery legs
    and did an obscene can-can on billboards across the prairie;
In the era when letters of the alphabet ballooned from our mouths,
    becoming a cloud of locusts blocking out the sun...

        ...a little light please,
        a sandgrain,
        silence.

Let the heaviness of noise fall from me like handfuls of hair,
    like a skin of insects, a set of teeth,
    like my body sliding off yours cools all of summer's madness;
Let the walls of noise crumble in a final demolition
    of temples, palaces, pyramids, skyscrapers, prisons;
Let the rich suits of noise be chewed to a silken dust
    by a cosmic release of moths;
Let the appliances of noise be served up like hearts
    on a black stone in the Temple of the Sun.

Oh my cold white, salt frozen angels,
Man is a city blaring with red alarms;
let his throat be a highway
    on which nothing but your light feet walk
            cutting off his speech.

STEVE ABBOTT

AFTER READING CATULLUS

I have run after those boys
they with flippant heads, posing
as gods or sacred wrynecks aflutter.
I would elevate them on a pedestal
alright, & hoist them up for all to admire
(O down to Faith's last drop I would)
but I have lost confidence in this religion.
Today it is not bodies or even love men worship
but some oblique gamesmanship, some mime
wherein we pretend to court gods none believe.
It's as if the temple were hung with rags
behind which stand no trace of any word
but word of mouth, & that
from the biggest liar in town.

Yet I rejoice! My heart
is calm & afterwards in the countryside
I have learned to love myself.

WALKING THIS ABANDONED FIELD

Walking this abandoned field I am looking
for something inside myself, an old
shovel perhaps or some evidence of planted seed.
I come upon a tree
much like one I used to climb as a boy
& lying down, my eyes
roam over the frayed hatband of evening sky.

This is how I used to feel loving you.
How sweet the air smelled then, like rain
in Nebraska after a field was plowed.
Now all I can see is this tree
& the memory of how high we once climbed.

ROBERT DUNCAN

PREFACE TO THE SUITE

1

Childhood, boyhood, young manhood
ached at the heart with it,   the unnameable,
the incompletion of desires,   and at the margins
shook.   O Wind, South Wind,   dark
and laden with long awaited rains,
in me a likeness that is yours   sings
—always sang—and now that manhood has grown full
and half a century of the seasons rehearsed,
again, again, adolescent to what new man,
you come in dreams and to the margins of my thought
stray.

      O Need, beloved Adversary to Love's settlements,
Invader, the halcyon days are over.
A violent season tears the depth of the blue.
The kingfisher turns from his studies where
his nature grows disquiet in him,   some
wildness of a winter is all his, and
looks out upon the alterd scene it belongs to,
hunting.

      Today belongs to you, to the music
about to be heard, the distant luring call recalld,
the strain, the estrangement from all I knew,
another knowledge straining to be free.

O deepest Unrest, indelibly engraved in me,
the wilderness beyond the edge of town, the riverbottom road,
the lingering, the wandering, the going astray,
to find some wanton promise the derelict landscape most portrayd in me,
the fog's sad density of cold,
in me, the solitary and deserted paths,
in me, the marshy wastes, the levee road
where day after day as if driven by the wind
I impatient strode,   day driven after day,
until the rush of impending weather was most me

in me, the dumb about-to-be, the country way
incapable of speech driven toward impending speech.

I was never there.   He was never there.
In some clearing before I reacht it
or after I was gone,   some *he*
had laid him down to sleep   where Pan
under his winter sun had roused the wildness with his song,
and, long lingering,
the air was heavy with his absence there—
Lord of the Heat of Noon still palpable
where late shadows chill the dreaming land.

2

Ghosts and lovers of my sixteenth year, old themes
and changing keys of a persisting music,
here, the colors fade,   I cannot recall the face,   there,
some pattern revivifies the scheme.   What
was the accurate contour of the fathering dream?

The year my father died died into me and dyed
anew the green of green, the gold gold shone from,
the blue that colors seas and skies to speak
of sadness innocence most knew,   and into Man
a mystery to take the place of fatherhood he grew
in me, a ghostly   bridegroom fathering his bride in me,
an emptiness in which an absence I call *You*
was present,   a pride,   a bright unanswering bliss,
consumed my heart.   It was a fiery ghost,
a burning substitution darkening all the sexual ways,
striving in those urgencies to speak,   to speak,
to heal unutterable injuries.   It was a wounded mouth,
a stricken thing unable to release its word,
a panic spring no youthful coming could exhaust in me.

DEVORAH MAJOR

AFRICAN COSMOLOGY

In that place
in that time
when the seeds we swallowed
planted themselves
in moist red folds
began to suck sweet womb juices
to grow root veins
translucent skins
Pushed out our bellies in mounds
that undulated life as we bent
over spring seedlings

When the birth entrails
were bathed in palm wine
buried in moss filled
earthen altars beneath
babobab trees spawned from
feces of orangutan bowels
in that time
when seasons' comings
reflected clocks time
and seasons' passing
recorded time's ignorance

In that age when god was found
in flowing river beds' algae
sung to on stretched goat skins
bathed in blood and milk
from a white haired ewe
Then we understood life
as an undying seed
cousin to the wind
child of the ocean
mother of the earth

In that place
in that time
in that humid sweated

plant filled land
of birth and passing
rebirth and changes
Cycles/worlds unseen
and remembered
in candlelit ceremony
we knew not death
and we could not
be destroyed.

UNTITLED LOVE

loving
        you
is riding a star
        my fingers hot
        sparks
is an avalanche crushing
        lungs
            cutting
dreams   is
loose belly folds
        flesh
is damp moss
        pressed to my nose

JAMES NOLAN

UNDERCURRENT

One afternoon the sea
slipped into his ear
and it was all he could hear,
the rush of the tides,
his head to a conch
of bells and fog horns
and that is why

he only half listened,
that is really why
he was ony half there,
half with the rattle
of tongues and milk trucks
and half with the sea
in his ear.

Listen, they said,
your ear's stopped up,
and then tried to make
his ear go pop and
they locked him up and
they let him out but
it would not stop

and he washed through a life
that seemed a lot like
the lives all around him
wearing a vague stereo-
phrenic smile while
he churned with the currents
and was thrashed by the rhythms

growing louder and louder
until it was all he could hear,
all he could bear, and no one,
not a single one believed
that his head was filled
by the motioning ocean

but they believed the trail
of words the drowning man left,
cupped words, resonant as shells,

and were astonished as they
held them to their ears.

RICHARD RONAN

THE WOMAN WHO KEPT
THE BOY WHO KEPT CATS

The sex over and done, we were, more or less,
    a charcoal ladder
        of coals.
When the breeze blew, his back glimmered up,
an orange rash of stars,
        mean-eyed in the dark,
    a thousand cats awakened in the future
    by the slit-eyed scent of rain.

We'd come to the cliffs again,
        leapt at each other's thighs
    and, in free fall, infinite and deep fall,
    committed again our infinite disregard
        for living long.
    Bones rung, singing like hammerheads
    struck on pads, muscle
            harder than bone,
    on skin stuck with the garment of tongues
            and juices.

And this time we broke the face
        of that wall of friends within,
    so fearful of our well-being,
        our audience of aunts;
he chewed my hard nipples raw,
    splintered a hip
        climbing on, in and out of me.
Then it went quick past pain,
    the fast male rush at the white circle
where pain lays out her silks
to be stolen or stained;
          then this
            long, long apocalypse
        where I'm wondering wide, wondering down:
        how could I have opened his back
    like that with my fingers,
        so that it looks like a bird
        had dug there, a dog

after the ass-end scent of his heart,
            and not have *known* it,
         neither he nor I,
so seized or suspended were we, so fire-mouthed.

Before he fell asleep between my legs,
            and became this impossible weight
      pulled by some magnet whose line runs from his thick body
            through mine to the center of a molten earth,
                  he said to my belly
                  that he'd kept cats
                  as a boy
            in milk boxes, a dovecote, bags sometimes;

      that he and his dimwit brother hunted them,
      lured them with cream and slabs of fish
      and put them inside
      where they went wild with gut yowling
            and vicious hisses,

just to see them change, hear them change
from slow paws and pussies to a knot of claws
            and piss-white hatred,
      to sit quite close beside them while they tried
      to cut out his eyes,
                  to soft-talk them
                  some sweet trash and tell them
                  that he loved them.

A SIGHTING OF WHALES

Irish moss thick on the coastal scrub
like a blossoming head of smoke,
the vast tilted crossings of road
and rocky meadow,
the patterns of tame animals—cow, horse, sheep.
Behind, the city in its chill mist and violet light.
Noon sun over all, white in the dense haze,
high clouding, slate-colored in part,
patches of bright uncolored sunlight
moving from the towers of business

to the bay across madrona grove and redwood,
farms and seal rocks, to the sea and the passages
of the sea and past the sea.
And this is the world as it is,
and our lesson is entry into it.

We watch in an odd kind of quiet,
lining cliffs and steps, the lighthouse rockery
and railings, staring to all sides, in pairs and trios,
some into the apocalyptic corridor of glare
where the colorless sun is sliding down its thread
to seawater in silver flame far below,
watching for the sudden spume,
the surfacing brow and back, the vast lift of tail,
perhaps for the special shock of their breaking,
a leap of one, two, three vast lives
in balletic series, rising for a moment
into the endless blur of light, water, warm air,
wind, into the feeling of connection and awe.

One blows, another nuzzling beside
a moment later, our fixed community suddenly stilled,
one or two pointing to the left of the brightest glare,
instructing others, palms to eyes—
then a break, a *leap*, electrical,
and all of us are applauding, shouting, in tears,
near blind with the day of waiting, with gratitude.

We are those who have waited,
ruined faith, broken eye,
alone in the terror of a natureless world,
seeking to know how to know, see how to see,
some bent to seedlings and moss,
others to the leviathan and its young
as they follow a warmth in the waters
toward the place they were born.

Seabirds lift and settle again, white among rocks,
lost in patterns of foam, winding lace-like
at stone footings.
The twin creatures show once again,
modestly, briefly, in the full, terrible glare
where the light makes of them dark silhouettes,
mottled, difficult to look at,
little more than a sense of large movement,
a double plume of spray.

GACELA

if lorca wanted
to die
heaving
with the boy
on the ship's deck
if he wanted
to be stiller
than death
will allow
and
if this were
the singing
of the sea
harping
in his ear
constantly
and
echoing also
out of the shell
of the boy's heart
and
the hearts
of other boys
and
if the sweet child
stood still
like a hindoo
and dug after
the rasping
in his chest
again and again
with a fork
or a spoon
or any implement
so anxious
was he
to hit bottom
and if lorca
saw this
rerun endlessly
like a skipping
syllable
then I too

have wishes
and
seas so high
they are skies

sometimes
there is
something
like his
in me—
my eye
I think.
I think
my eye is
hauling groceries
home for
my grandmother
and
there's a lame wheel
on its cart
that yips
and sticks
and fishtails.
I think
my eye
wants to retreat
back
to the chipped
sound of
the wheel
back
into the head
elbowing
back
brokenly
panicked
like a bird
unable to use
wings
back
through all the
delicate
brainworks

to the
fluorescence
of first-thought
to the regular
waves
that are particles
to the particles
misbehaving
as wave
to ions
hung
in the
brain air.
I think my eye
wants to descend
the quantum staircase
with the sweet boy
and his spoon
and step-to
with him
down
until
we are
kissing
in awesome
silence.

there
the air will
roar
like a heart.
only one
mouth
will
be engaged
in our kiss
and
it will have
no word
to share.
yes
to die with
him—
to die
at every touch
of him—
to die
down
until we
come out
the other shore
trailing
seaweed and fear

"THE TURQUOISE HORSE RIDING"

the turquoise horse riding
on your mouth
the ice horse broken
in your heat
I have heard whole seasons
in your steps
toward my bed
your hairs each eclipse
the several phases
of the moon

EUGENE RUGGLES

A WOMAN INSIDE EL SALVADOR

"Let us walk together outside the night
of repression and hunger and intervention . . ."
Carlos Fuentes

She is taking the corn tortilla
from a table of planks before her,
murmuring to herself and the leaf of corn—
The living are too used to life.
The ones up north. Even here.
They are soaked with it. They close around it.
The young will not do this any longer;
they are closer to death than life,
they have grown so quickly
in this soil of death their roots
are before them—Last night
she went to the city for money,
for the last time, her fingers
smell of men, she is done with living
from her body. She fills a wooden bowl
with water from a pail
and stands up,
pulling the needles of sleep
from her eyelids.
She was born in 1932,
lifted from a flood of 30,000 peasants
shot to death, the *matanza* of February 1932;
the volcanoes of El Salvador
filled with blood in 1932.
The morning begins to thicken
until she can see the tongue prints
of men filling with dust,
the tanks of Washington gasoline
filling the death squads.
The street dogs shake off
their flies. The huts begin to inhale
through the holes in their walls.
So many heavy boots
laced with wires and veins,
knotted with echoes from the north
and coated with a century of ashes

are falling from her back
as she stands up;
insects crawl into them—
They have given us a stone
for a window and leaves
for the stones to rebuild our walls.
There is only one country on earth,
all wars are civil wars—
Light falls down the dark well
of her long hair and remembers.
She listens to the Archbishop kneeling,
the fourteen holes in his chest deepening
from the bullets of the fourteen families,
the fountains rising from them.
She moves her finger along the scar
that is in every ear of corn
to be eaten...
Monsignor, Monsignor, Monsignor.
Her feet are naked
as water,
when she walks outside
into her country, its young cemeteries,
the poor, their marriage, her cathedral.

San Francisco, December, 1983

THE LIFEGUARD IN THE SNOW

It seems the snow is falling deeper than God
as I walk through it along our end of the ice,
it drifts between my legs like it was breathing.
The sweat hits in my back as I start to climb
the first white dunes that save the trees from ice,
I open my coat and hear snow inhaling the lake.
There is the raft I couldn't reach it's still there
frozen in ice like the last scream in a mouth.
Watching those young children all last summer
has folded this black sunburn through my chest—
a small girl water carved out of my arms forever.

LIGHTING THE OCEANS

The world's seas cannot be expected to survive the present oil ships...
We'll find something else instead of oil to turn our too-many wheels.
The seas we shan't replace.

—Noel Mostert, *Supership*

The herds of buffalo
may be dead,
but the herds of oil
are only beginning to roam
the oceans,
trampling the gills and feathers
to death.

Remember only a few waves ago
how the pores in our skin,
after the scales and feathers
were lifted from them,
began to sing...

These new herds graze faster
behind their great tankers
where the captains of Standard
would never walk,
clogging the sands
whenever the waves can throw them off.

We could tie them with fire
as they revolve
so the last sea people
can turn away
in time
from our waste
we could heat the oceans this winter.

The owners agree
and wipe their ships down
with oceans,
if need be with war,
for they have already drilled
into the tongue
and found nothing of value.

And each season
as women know,

the moon will dig for its tides
with less strength
through this black ice upon white ice,
through these graves that we sail.

THE UNEMPLOYED AUTOMOBILE WORKERS OF DETROIT PREPARE TO SHARE CHRISTMAS STANDING IN LINE

It's December. Nearly Christmas. Nineteen Eighty-three.
The Detroit River is choked with ice. Woodward Avenue
is empty of automobiles and flowing with a foot of snow.
The snow drifts under the doors and into the taverns
along Highland Park. This is the spine of Detroit
where the snow turns grey as it nears the factories.
It's nine a.m. as I enter a bar near Grand Boulevard,
the jukebox is dark, a woman drinking leans into it.
The bar is long and empty, a bartender hands me a glass,
saying he's been waiting months for G.M. to call him back.
A black man comes in to cash his unemployment check.
He's at my right elbow, looking down, signing his name.
He has four children to feed, today. He turns to ask
if I want to shoot a game of pool. We flip a coin
to see who breaks. He wins. I was born around here,
forty-two years ago today, just before Pearl Harbor.
The last of five children from parents who never sang,
they broke their lives over each other until they ended.
The snow never stops looking for men in Detroit.
It spreads out through the suburbs and small towns
to the farms up north looking for men, closing roads.
It hires them in the spring and summer delivers them
to a landlord, a woman, their children. Fall is whiskey.
The oil drains to the bottom of the machinery. Gears lock.
This is December. I lift up a glass. So does he. Here is
to the five horses grazing at the end of your wrist.

STEVE SILBERMAN

from RECONSECRATING GROUND ZERO

Cant take our bodies
when the bomb lets us in
cant take hearing cant take eyesight
when the bomb opens,
cant take John Kennedy,
cant take the trail up the silent mountain,
cant return prettier, more peaceful
to tend the garden
when the sparrow flies up
in the thorny courtyard,
cant go back home
cant go back home
cant buy out, cant change the election,
cant storm the fences with suitcases of proof
when the chain of command,
when the executives rush to the elevators
for the trade-off,
when the first strike squadron enters Soviet airspace,
cant reswallow our souls
at the moment of detonation
cant recoronate the lamb on the heart's throne
and pardon the Thief, when the bomb opens
its flower of heavy elements

AT A VFW SQUAREDANCE IN GREYSON COUNTY

Skinny, in a white cap, shirt unbuttoned,
shot-up tall—he caught
me staring at him
under the smoking lights of the dance.
Soon he's sitting in the chair next to mine:
"Do y'drink? Now I mean likker.
C'mon!" Out the door to the parking lot,
an open truck
in the needle frost.
A brown paper bag on the seat, full of Dinkel's whiskey.

ALTA

from VETERANS' DAY IN HEALDSBURG

healdburg's such a
nest: wood frame
houses, tree-shaded
lawns, the diner, the
school, & above
the school, the town
cemetery, where arnold
nicker lies dead, &
matt plays the flute.

travel must
sound so exciting
to these working-
class boys with so
little chance of
seeing the world.
viet nam must
have sounded like
such an adventure.

*

rob's story:

i was hit, & everybody around me
was blown open—& then these guys,
chattering stuff i couldnt understand:
the one thing i was deathly afraid of was,
i was gonna snore.   i always snore when i'm
on my back, but when i fell, i fell on my
stomach.   i was only hit in one spot; i was
all covered with blood & guts—that's the only
thing that saved me. they figured it came from me.

movies dont sound anything like my experience.
it's quiet—only every so often, bang bang,
& then, clink clink clink of bayonets.

so i lay absolutely still for two days. just
lay there, praying i wouldnt snore. & i wasnt
even a soldier!   i was over there working for the
phone company!

*

damian's a vege-
tarian.   he says,
ever since viet
nam, he cant
stomach meat.

*

damian keeps a loaded shotgun
in the trunk of his car. when
i bitch that vegetarians dont
like killing, he says, "anybody
touches my stuff, i'll blow him away!"

*

DRAFT RESISTOR: pat's story

the food in jail wasnt so bad.
in fact, i thought it was great!
chocolate pudding, tapioca—
stuff i hadnt seen
since i was a kid!

the worst part was
all that bad american coffee.

JOHN OLIVER SIMON

80 SHEETS NARROW RULE

O your freeways, your polluted rivers!
A man in buckskin circumnavigates the nation chanting.
Shot in real time, the dude in the mirror
sure gets polite all of a sudden.
The road reflects the surface of the moon.
This nostrilled one will never learn.
Talk show, turquoise, blare of smog.

Most of the stores in the arcade are out of business.
Looks like a quarterback drop into the ice age.
I don't want to be brusque in disagreeing
but still I'd rather extricate myself.
Turn off the highway south of the cemetery.
Run naked through the sagebrush till you see the morning star.

PAULA GUNN ALLEN

ELEGY FOR MY SON

I wanted to write 1968 for today's date—as though
somewhere between then and
then, some step taken could be untaken, or a word
spoken be unsaid
some little thing done
not
wouldn't lead into
where with bewildered hands I sit
holding your small body dead.

MOUNTAIN SONG

Let
me sprinkle pollen on your head
tell
the tales that hold the rocks to life

I
will walk
nobly to Black Mesa
lost to the redstone gate
of dawn.

The treacherous
pot-holes are drunk
with clouds.

(The enemy
has many wiles)

HE NA TYE WOMAN

Water.
Lakes and rivers.
Oceans and streams.
Springs, pools and gullies.
Arroyos, creeks, watersheds.
Pacific. Atlantic. Mediterranean.
Indian. Caribbean. China Sea.
(Lying. Dreaming on shallow shores.)
Arctic. Antarctic. Baltic.
Mississippi. Amazon. Columbia. Nile.
Thames. Sacramento. Snake. (undulant woman river.)
Siene. Rio Grande. Willamette. McKenzie. Ohio.
Hudson. Po. Rhine. Rhone.
Rain. After a lifetime of drought.
That finally cleanses the air.
The soot from our eyes.
The dingy windows of our western home.
The rooftops and branches. The wings of birds.
The new light on a slant. Pouring. Making everything new.

Water (woman) that is the essence of you.
He na tye (woman) that is recognition and remembering.
Gentle. Soft. Sure.
Long shadows of afternoon, growing as the light turns
west toward sleep. Turning with the sun.

(The rest of it is continents and millenia.
 How could I have waited so long for completion?)

The water rises around us like the goddess coming home.
(Arisen.) Same trip, all things considered, all times
and visions, all places and spaces taken into account
on that ancient journey, finally returned. The maps, the plans,
the timetables: the carefully guided tours into all manner
of futilities. Manners the last turn in the road: arid irony.

(Lady, why does your love so touch me?
(Lady, why do my hands have strength for you?
(Lady, how could I wander so long without you?

Water in Falls, misting and booming on the rocks below.
Tall pines in the mist, the deep carved caves.
Water in rivulets. Gathering speed, drops joining in headlong flight.

Unnamed rivers, flowing eternally underground,
     unchanging, unchanged.
Water thundering down long dry arroyos, the ancient causeways
of our faith. Drought over, at last. Carrying silt,
bits of broken glass, branches, pebbles, pieces of abandoned cars,
parts of lost houses and discarded dreams. Downstream.
Storms of water, and we
deluged
singing
hair plastered to our ecstatic skulls,
waving wild fists at the bolts hurled at us from above
teeth shimmering in the sheets of rain (the sheen)
eyes blinded with the torrents that fall fromthroughover them:
Rain. The Rain that makes us new.
That rain is you.
How did I wait so long to drink.

SNOWGOOSE

North of here where
water marries ice,
meaning is other than what
I understand.

I have seen in picture how
white the bulge of the glacier
overshadows the sea,
frozen pentecostal presence,
brilliant in the sun —
way I have never been.

I heard the snowgoose cry today
long-wheeled wings overhead,
sky calling untroubled blue
song to her and morning.
(North wind blowing.)

GREGORY CORSO

THE WHOLE MESS...ALMOST

I ran up six flights of stairs
to my small furnished room
opened the window
and began throwing out
those things most important in life

First to go, Truth, squealing like a fink:
"Don't! I'll tell awful things about you!"
"Oh yeah? Well, I've got nothing to hide...OUT!"
Then went God, glowering & whimpering in amazement:
"It's not my fault! I'm not the cause of it all!" "OUT!"
Then Love, cooing bribes: "You'll never know impotency!
All the girls on *Vogue* covers, all yours!"
I pushed her fat ass out and screamed:
"You always end up a bummer!"
I picked up Faith Hope Charity
all three clinging together:
"Without us you'll surely die!"
"With you I'm going nuts! Goodbye!"

Then Beauty...ah, Beauty—
As I led her to the window
I told her: "You I loved best in life
...but you're a killer; Beauty kills!"
Not really meaning to drop her
I immediately ran downstairs
getting there just in time to catch her
"You saved me!" she cried
I put her down and told her: "Move on."

Went back up those six flights
went to the money
there was no money to throw out.
The only thing left in the room was Death
hiding beneath the kitchen sink:
"I'm not real!" It cried
"I'm just a rumor spread by life..."

Laughing I threw it out, kitchen sink and all
and suddenly realized Humor
was all that was left—
All I could do with Humor was to say:
"Out the window with the window!"

H. DAVID MOE

FREE

free of clouded sinews
   path to the beginnings horizon layed before you
free of the giant small average of the people
   touch the gong of tears moment
free of taught cycles & inherent absolutes
   open the bubbletop of your bailiwick listening continuum
free of the unconscious assumptions puppeting you along
   the same nowhere
     divedeep & turnaround observing the projectionist
     behind your thoughts
free of painful times & epiphany heights of remembrance
   occur to yourself monotony extending you in engendered
   beautiful nothingness
free of spontaneous livelies intoxicated fugue of choices
    out there
     lay back & let your genetics do it
free of the prison utopia of your most tested and caressed
    weltanschauung
      crystal ice is the mind to the rising sun on a meadow
free of searching, hide
free of ordering, create
free of doubt, question
free of butter, sapphire
free of breath, spin into the waves, feel the pulling red cup
    solarplexus to the centering wings of the earth
free of all
    zero point undifferential angled unto exact opposite

VICTOR HERNÁNDEZ CRUZ

THE SWANS' BOOK

In my neighborhood I saw two swans take a taxi
because they got bored of the mirror they had them in
Year in and year out they bought flowers in front of them
The mirror reflected the red the orange but the swans
couldn't touch the blues   so they got bored like
an unfound book in an abandoned building in the
South Bronx
One swan said to the other:
Who are these hypocrites who have parties and
throw rum in our faces?
They look like coffee percolators with their
excitement
We can't live, only look at it
I want outs, I'm gonna unglue off of this heated
sand and make for the door
I agree, said the other swan, and they peeled
off the glass mirror from the corner where
they decorated   spread their white wings once
and out the door they swayed
Each floor they passed had a different smell
Like one floor smelled sweet like bananas
The next one smelled like tamarind
The next one like incense
They marched past the people on the stoop
who in a state of shock froze like winter snow
You see things in the world, one said
A pedestrian looked so deep his eyes went out of
his face like on wheels
But the swans were into their thing
and that corner was for them like cake from
the oven and if they saw the owner of the
mirror they'd tell him where it was at
To hell with living motionless
suffering nonproblems having delusions
worrying about everything
just pressed against a wall that belongs to
a landlord who never comes in the winter to
understand cold
Watching people dance, all kinds of formations

Every rhythm gots a dance
People eat white beans and don't offer
The odors were killing us
To hell with being the swans decorating the
right-hand corners of mirrors
Everyone says how beautiful we look
and then ignores us like some inanimate object
Lulu to those who will see the blank we leave
behind
Now that we gone the city will turn gray
The residents will fight
from seeing too much nothing sitting next to each other
We don't want to be microphones for someone who
combs their hair with Dixie Peach and sings tragic
bolero blues about broken hearts and impossible loves
while a toothpick hangs from their mouth
That's right, that it is, gasoline with this place
On the corner they flopped their wings
A big taxi came to them
They sailed in like keys into a lock
When the taxi sped away from the neighborhood
one wing came out of each of the side windows
The crowd that mingled noticed the swans
escape
The yellow metal elevated into the air
dwindling into a dot
as the residents chit chat about the spectacle
One of them pops:
Now it's our turn to wake up
A loud voice was heard in the eardrum
Hey, wake up
before that mirror falls on your head

THREE SONGS FROM THE 50's

Song 1

Julito used to shine the soul
of his shoes before he left for
the Palladium to take the wax
off the floor while Tito Rodriguez
flew around the walls like a

parakeet choking maracas
It was around this time that
Julito threw away his cape
because the Umbrella Man and the
Dragons put the heat on all the
Ricans who used to fly around
in Dracula capes swinging canes
or carrying umbrellas
Even if there was no rain
on the horizon
That same epoca my mother
got the urge to paint the
living room pink and buy a
new mirror with flamingoes
elegantly on the right hand
corner because the one we had
was broken from the time that
Carlos tried to put some respect
Into Julito and knock the
party out of him.

Song 2

All the old Chevies that the
gringoes from upstate New York
wore out
Were sailing around the neighborhood
with dices and San Martin de Porres
el negrito who turned catholic
Hanging in the front windows.

Song 3

There was still no central heating
in the tenements
We thought that the cold was
the oldest thing on the planet earth
We used to think about my Uncle Listo
Who never left his hometown
We'd picture him sitting around
cooling himself with a fan
In that imaginary place
called Puerto Rico.

BOB KAUFMAN

THE POET

FROM A PIT OF BONES
THE HANDS OF CREATION
FORM THE MIND, AND SHAPE
THE BODY IN LESS THAN A SECOND.
    A FISH WITH FROG'S
    EYES,
    CREATION IS PERFECT.
THE POET NAILED TO THE
BONE OF THE WORLD
COMES IN THROUGH A DOOR,
TO LIVE UNTIL
HE DIES,
WHATEVER HAPPENS IN BETWEEN,
IN THE NIGHT OF THE LIVING
DEAD, THE POET REMAINS ALIVE,
    A FISH WITH FROG'S
    EYES,
    CREATION IS PERFECT.
THE POET WALKS ON THE EARTH
AND OBSERVES THE SILENT
SPHINX UPON THE NILE.
THE POET KNOWS HE MUST
WRITE THE TRUTH,
EVEN IF HE IS
KILLED FOR IT, FOR THE
SPHINX CANNOT BE DENIED.
WHENEVER A MAN DENIES IT,
A MAN DIES.
THE POET LIVES IN THE
MIDST OF DEATH
AND SEEKS THE MYSTERY OF
LIFE, A STONE REALITY IN THE
REALM OF SYMBOLS, FANTASY, AND
METAPHOR, FOR REASONS
THAT ARE HIS OWN WHAT IS REAL
IS THE PIT OF BONES HE COMES

FROM,
    A FISH WITH FROG'S
    EYES,
    CREATION IS PERFECT.
SOMEWHERE A BUDDHA SITS IN
SILENCE AND HOLDS THE
POET AND THE WORLD IN
SEPARATE HANDS AND REALIZES HE
IS BORN TO
DIE.
THE BLOOD OF THE POET
MUST FLOW IN HIS POEM,
SO MUCH SO, THAT OTHERS
DEMAND AN EXPLANATION.
THE POET ANSWERS THAT THE
POEM IS NOT TO BE
EXPLAINED. IT IS WHAT IT
IS, THE REALITY OF THE POEM
CANNOT BE DENIED,
    A FISH WITH FROG'S
    EYES,
    CREATION IS PERFECT.
THE POET IS ALONE WITH OTHERS
LIKE HIMSELF. THE PAIN IS BORN
INTO THE POET. HE MUST LIVE
WITH IT. IT IS HIS SOURCE OF
PURITY, SUFFERING HIS
LEGACY,
THE POET HAS TO BE A
STONE.
    A FISH WITH FROG'S
    EYES,
    CREATION IS PERFECT.
WHEN THE POET PROTESTS THE
DEATH HE SEES AROUND
HIM,
THE DEAD WANT HIM SILENCED.
HE DIES LIKE LORCA DID,
YET LORCA SURVIVES IN HIS
POEM, WOVEN INTO THE DEEPS
OF LIFE. THE POET SHOCKS THOSE
AROUND HIM. HE SPEAKS OPENLY
OF WHAT AUTHORITY HAS DEEMED

UNSPEAKABLE, HE BECOMES THE
ENEMY OF AUTHORITY. WHILE THE
POET LIVES, AUTHORITY
DIES. HIS POEM IS
FOREVER.
WHEN THE POET DIES,
A STONE IS PLACED ON
HIS GRAVE, IT IS HIM,
A PIT OF BONES,
    CREATION IS PERFECT,
IN THE PIT OF BONES
A SKY OF STARS, A HEAVEN OF
SUNS AND MOONS, AND THE GREAT
SUN IN THE CENTER,
    CREATION IS PERFECT.
A MASK CREATED IN THE PIT
IS THE IMAGE OF THE POET.
THE IMAGE OF THE POET
IS A
SECRET.
    A FISH WITH FROG'S
    EYES,
    CREATION IS PERFECT.
I HAVE WALKED IN THIS WORLD
WITH A CLOAK OF DEATH WRAPPED
AROUND ME. I WALKED ALONE, EVERY
KISS WAS A WOUND, EVERY SMILE
A THREAT.
ONE DAY DEATH REMOVED HIS
CAPE FROM AROUND ME,
I UNDERSTOOD WHAT I HAD LIVED
THROUGH. I HAD NO REGRETS,
WHEN THE CLOAK WAS REMOVED,
I WAS IN A PIT OF BONES,
    A FISH WITH FROG'S
    EYES,
    CREATION IS PERFECT.

BIOGRAPHICAL NOTES

STEVE ABBOTT studied poetry with Karl Shapiro and John Berryman and taught writing at the U. of Nebraska and Emory University. He has published three books of poetry, edited *Poetry Flash* from 1979-85, as well as the magazine *Soup*, 1980-85. He's read at the One World Poetry Festival in Amsterdam and the Village Voice Bookstore in Paris. He currently teaches writing at the University of San Francisco.

FRANCISCO X. ALARCÓN, Chicano poet, critic and editor, recently moved to Santa Cruz from San Francisco, where he lived for the past seven years in the Latino Mission District. He is now a visiting lecturer in the Spanish for Spanish-Speakers Program at the University of California Santa Cruz. He has published two collections of poetry, *Ya Vas, Carnal*, and *Tattoos*. He is editor of *The Literary Magazine* of *El Tecolote*, a bilingual newspaper published by the community in San Francisco. He has been the recipient of Danforth and Fulbright Fellowships. He is writing his Ph.D. dissertation at Stanford University.

FERNANDO ALEGRÍA is a Chilean in exile. His most recent of several volumes of poetry is his selected poems, *Changing Centuries*, translated by Stephen Kessler. He has written a number of novels and much criticism, mostly on Latin American fiction. He has edited the anthology *Chilean Writers in Exile*. He served as Chilean cultural attaché in the United States during the Allende administration, and is now professor of Spanish and Latin American Literature at Stanford University.

PAULA GUNN ALLEN is of Laguna Pueblo/Sioux/Lebanese American descent. She was born in Albuquerque and raised in Cubero, New Mexico. Her work includes a novel, *The Woman Who Owned The Shadows*; a collection of essays, *The Sacred Hoop: Recovering the Feminine in American Indian Traditions*; several chapbooks; and the book of poems, *Shadow Country*. She was awarded a grant by the NEA in 1978. She recently completed a new book of poems, *Skins and Bones*, and is at work on a Medicine Dyke novel.

ALTA is the founder and publisher of Shameless Hussy Press. She has lived in the Bay Area for 31 of her 43 years. She has published 12 books of poetry and prose. She is currently at work on a book of poems on new and selected lovers.

ROBERT ANBIAN has published one collection of poetry, *Bohemian Airs & Other Kefs* (Night Horn Books, 1982). He has variously described himself as "a rat who failed his Skinner box" and "a rather depressing character." He works as an editor in San Francisco.

ROGER APLON was born and raised in Chicago and began writing in his early twenties. He was the managing editor of CHOICE Magazine with John Logan and Aaron Siskind from 1961 through the seventies. His work was anthologized in Paul Carroll's *The Young American Poets*. He has taught at the University of Hawaii and Columbia College in Chicago. His two volumes of poetry are *Stiletto* and *By Dawn's Early Light at 120 Miles Per Hour.* He recently opened a restaurant in San Francisco, 39 Grove.

JANICE BLUE was born and raised in Western Kentucky, of English and Scot root, with a little Chicksaw and German as well. She has lived in San Francisco some twenty years. "I write in idiom, street lingo, and more than a few southern talks, also hipster and carny. . . . I don't believe schools have anything to teach creative languages or the changing and totally ignored older tongues of our land." She was born New Year's Day, 1942. Her first book of poems was *In Good Old No-Man's Land.*

KAREN BRODINE is a typesetter and political activist. She has taught creative writing at San Francisco State. A founding member of Kelsey St. Press and the Women Writers Union in San Francisco, her work has appeared in many left, feminist and gay/lesbian publications. Her three books of poetry are *Slow Juggling,* *Workweek,* and *Illegal Assembly.* She is a member of Radical Women.

JAMES BROUGHTON has been a lively influence on the San Francisco scene since 1948 when his first book, *The Playground,* and his first film, *Mother's Day,* appeared. Since then he has produced some twenty books and as many films, has received two Guggenheim Fellowships, two grants from the NEA, and a Cannes Festival Award for *The Pleasure Garden.* His major books are *A Long Undressing, Seeing The Light,* and *Ecstasies.* In the world of cinema he is most famous for *Loony Tom* and *The Bed.* He claims to be a confirmed believer in the amatory, the hilarious and the unmentionable.

D.F. BROWN was born in Springfield, Missouri in 1948 on April Fools Day. After an obligatory adolescence there, he served as a medic with the Fourth Infantry Division in the central highlands of Vietnam in 1969-70. He has two children and works as a night nurse in the heart ward. His first collection, *Returning Fire,* was the 1984 San Francisco State University Poetry chapbook.

JANINE CANAN was born in Los Angeles in 1942. She graduated from Stanford, studied German Literature at the University of California, and was a teacher for nine years. She received her M.D. from New York University School of Medicine and is a practicing psychiatrist in Berkeley. She has published five books of poetry, the most recent of which is *Her Magnificent Body, New and Selected Poems,* from ManRoot Books. Her work has appeared in the anthologies *New Directions 42, New Lesbian Writing,* and *State of Peace: The Women Speak.*

NEELI CHERKOVSKI was born in Santa Monica in 1945. His nine books of poetry include *Clear Wind, Love Proof, Public Notice,* and *The Juggler Within,* as well as *Ferlinghetti,* a biography of the poet Lawrence Ferlinghetti, published in 1979. He recently completed his first novel, *Angels Flight.* He edited the 20th anniversary issue of *Beatitude* Magazine.

ELLEN COONEY was born on June 23, 1948 in St. Louis, Missouri. She has published three books of poems: *The Silver Rose, The Quest for the Holy Grail*, and *House Holding*, and is at work on a fourth, *Within the Labyrinth All*. Her interests include medieval and renaissance music, history and world religions.

LUCHA CORPI was born in 1945 in Jáltipan, Veracruz. In 1964 she married and moved to live and study in Berkeley. She holds her B.A. from UC Berkeley and her M.A. from San Francisco State in Comparative Literature. In 1979 she was awarded a grant from the NEA. She lives in Oakland, where she teaches English as a second language in the public school system. Her two collections of poetry are *Firelight: Three Latin American Poets*, and *Palabras De Mediodía/Noon Words*.

GREGORY CORSO was born in NYC in 1930. Along with Allen Ginsberg, he was one of the major Beat poets. His titles include *The Happy Birthday of Death, Long Live Man, Elegiac Feelings American*, and *Herald of the Autochthonic Spirit*. He is the author of two plays and one novel, *The American Express*. "The poet and his poetry are inseparable."

VICTOR HERNÁNDEZ CRUZ was born in Aguas Buenas, Puerto Rico in 1949. His family moved to NYC in 1954. His four books of poems are *Snaps, Mainland, Tropicalization*, and *By Lingual Wholes*. "My family life was full of music, guitars and conga drums, maracas and songs. My work is on the border of a new language, because I create out of a consciousness steeped in two of the important world languages, Spanish and English. I write about the city with an agonizing memory of a lush tropical silence." He moved to San Francisco in the early 1970s. He has been a guest lecturer at UC Berkeley and an instructor at San Francisco State.

DIANE DI PRIMA has published twenty-one books of poetry and prose. Of these, the most recent include *Revolutionary Letters, Loba Parts 1-8*, and *Selected Poems: 1956-1975*. She was one of the founders of the New York Poets Theater and her own plays have been produced in New York, San Francisco and Los Angeles. She has been a member of the New College of California Poetics faculty since 1980, and has taught and read at universities throughout the United States. She also teaches privately in visualization, healing and the Western magical tradition.

KIRBY DOYLE was born in 1932. As a young poet he was influenced by Pound and Olson, later he was a student of Rexroth and drinking friend of Lew Welch. He has been in the U.S. Army, Orange and Marin County jails, and graduate school at San Francisco State. He has one novella and three books of poetry in print, including *The Collected Poems of Kirby Doyle*, from Greenlight Press. His early atheism is yet intact.

ROBERT DUNCAN was born in Oakland in 1919. He has been identified with the Black Mountain school of poetry and was deeply involved in the San Francisco Renaissance of the 1950s. He has lectured and read widely throughout the United States, Canada, Europe and Australia. In 1985 he was the recipient of The National Poetry Award for his lifetime achievements and devotion to poetry. His major titles include *The Opening of the Field, Roots and Branches, Bending the Bow*, and *Ground Work: Before the War*. Since 1951 he has lived with the painter Jess Collins.

LAURA FELDMAN, born in Portland, Oregon in 1954, author of *Cafe Songs*, lives in San Francisco. She works for Sierra Club Books.

LAWRENCE FERLINGHETTI is the founder and publisher of City Lights Books. His collection of poems, *A Coney Island of the Mind*, has sold over a million copies. His titles of poetry include *Starting from San Francisco, Landscapes of Living and Dying, Endless Life: Selected Poems*, and *Over All the Obscene Boundaries*. He is the author of several plays and the novel, *Her*. He recently published his travel journal, *Seven Days in Nicaragua Libre*.

GENE FOWLER was born in 1931 in Oakland. He served nearly five years in San Quentin for armed robbery, before becoming an "outlaw poet" in the sixties. His work has appeared in many little magazines and anthologies, including George Plimpton's first *American Literary Anthology*, Bill Henderson's first *Pushcart Prize Anthology*, and Robert Bly's *40 Poems On Recent American History*. His poetry titles include *FIRES: Selected Poems 1963-1976, Return of the Shaman*, and *The Quiet Poems*, as well as a "how to" on acquiring the poet's talents, *Waking the Poet*.

KATHLEEN FRASER lives in San Francisco where she teaches in the Creative Writing program at San Francisco State and edits the publication HOW(ever) for women poets writing from an experimentalist perspective. She received a grant from the NEA in 1979, and in 1981 she was awarded a Guggenheim. She started the American Poetry Archive at The Poetry Center at S.F. State in 1973. Her seven books of poetry include *What I Want, New Shoes, Something(even human voices)in the foreground, a lake*, and *Each Next*, a book of narratives. She is learning to speak Italian.

ROB GOLDSTEIN is the author of *Love Acts 25¢*, from Beaux Arts Press. His work has appeared in *No Apologies* and *Mirage*. He resides in San Francisco, where he lives and studies with Harold Norse.

RAFAEL JESÚS GONZÁLEZ was born and raised in El Paso, Texas. He was educated at the University of Texas at El Paso, Universidad Nacional Autónoma de México, and the University of Oregon. His first collection of poems was *El Hacedor De Juegos/The Maker of Games*. He currently teaches creative writing and literature at Laney College in Oakland.

JUDY GRAHN's most recent book of poems is *The Queen of Wands*, which won a Before Columbus Foundation American Book Award in 1982. Her poetry collection *The Work of a Common Woman* includes *The Common Woman Poems, She Who, Edward the Dyke*, and *A Woman Is Talking to Death*. She recently published a major work of Gay/Lesbian cultural history, *Another Mother Tongue: Gay Words, Gay Worlds*. She is at work on a new collection of poems, *The Queen of Swords*.

SUSAN GRIFFIN lives in Berkeley. Her poetry, fiction, essays, criticism and interviews have been widely published. Her titles include *Like the Iris of an Eye, Woman and Nature: The Roaring Inside Her, Pornography and Silence: Culture's Revenge Against*

Nature, and most recently, *Made From This Earth: An Anthology of Writings.* Her play, *Voices,* won an Emmy in 1975. She is at work on new collections of plays and poems. A book of essays, *The First and the Last: A Woman Thinks About War,* will be published by Doubleday.

THOM GUNN spent the first half of his life in Britain and the second in San Francisco, which makes him something of an amphibian among poets writing in English. His titles include *The Sense of Movement, Moly* and *My Sad Captains, Jack Straw's Castle, Selected Poems 1950-1975,* and his recent *The Passages of Joy.* His prose book, *The Occasions of Poetry: Essays and Autobiography,* was published in an enlarged edition by North Point Press in 1985.

KATHARINE HARER was born in Oakland in 1949. She has published three books of poetry: *Spring Cycle, In These Bodies,* and *The Border.* For three years she served as Executive Director of the California Poets-in-the-Schools program, and is currently the new Director of Small Press Traffic bookstore. She lives in San Francisco with Vern Maxam and their new son, Leo.

HOWARD HART was born in Ohio in 1927 and "got out via Paris and New York. Studied music with Charles Mills, philosophy with Herbert Schwartz. Have sought to know the best minds of my generation and the generations before and after me in the flesh if possible. Love jazz music. Have lived in Mexico, Morocco, Canada, Spain, Holland, England and France." His books include *Fountain Square, The Apple Bites Back,* and *Selected Poems: Six Sets, 1951-1983* (City Miner Books, P.O. Box 176, Berkeley, CA 94701).

JUAN FELIPE HERRERA recently went on a California tour with *Teatro Campesino.* He is a co-founder of *MediammiX,* a verbal art and rhythm performance ensemble. His titles are *Rebozos of Love, Exiles of Desire, A Night in Tunisia,* co-authored with Margarita Luna Robles, and the forthcoming *Akrilica,* from Alcatraz Editions. He has received NEA Writer's Fellowships in 1980 and 1985, and California Arts Council Artist-in-Communities grants in 1975, 1977 and 1983.

JACK HIRSCHMAN is an American communist cultural worker, author and translator of more than 55 books. He is a member of the Union of Left Writers, and of the cultural brigades named after poets Roque Dalton (El Salvador) and Jacques Roumain (Haiti). Along with his own prodigious output, he has translated from, among others: Antonin Artaud, Rene Depestre, Katerina Gogou, Stephan Mallarme, Pablo Neruda, and Luisa Pasamanik. He was born in New York City in 1933. His titles include *The David Arcane, Lyripol, Aur Sea, Black Aelphs,* and *The Proletarian Arcane.*

BOB KAUFMAN was born in New Orleans of mixed Black and Jewish parentage, one of fourteen children. A merchant marine for 20 years, he settled in California in the 1950s and spent several years in New York in the early 1960s. He neither spoke nor wrote for the ten years between John Kennedy's assassination and the signing of the Paris peace agreement in February 1973. His three books of poems are *Golden Sardine, Solitudes Crowded with Loneliness,* and *The Ancient Rain.* He died January 12, 1986.

MICHAEL KOCH was born in New York City in 1949, currently lives in Paris, and has travelled extensively in Latin America. He translates from both French and Spanish and is the author of *jamais*, from e.g. publications.

KUSH writes, "Born of Lillian & Sid in the Brooklyn Brain of the Great Fish of Long Island. I played ball on the moonfield of Bethpage. Illuminated by the Mohawk Valley, Hudson fed Bard and Mayan Museum of Krugers Island. Opened Cloud House on 72 Thompson St., Manhattan, charged by Walt Whitman to the poetry of presence. To air with my soul the Song of the Rolling Earth. Meditated on the continent, Turtle Island, at Palenque-Copan-Tikal-Monte Alban-Teotihuacan and brought this North with vows to awaken the States. Reading Walt Whitman & Planet Drum into the open air of 76 Philadelphia-Camden. Under the sign of Venus came West with Cloud House and opened The Nature Theater of San Francisco." He teaches anthropology at New College of California.

NANCY LAMBERT was born in Brooklyn and raised in New Jersey and Manhattan. "Grew up on Poe, Wells, the Brothers Grimm, grade-B science fiction flicks, Marvel Comics, and 7-Eleven slurpees and candy bars. A college drop-out (majoring in Jung, Kerouac, and post-adolescent angst via Plath and Hesse), I've worked as a bookstore manager, waitress, nanny, and chambermaid in NYC, San Francisco, L.A. and Tuscon." Her work has appeared in *The Little Magazine* and from Sea of Storms Press.

RICHARD LORANGER was born in 1960. "Raised in mid-mid-mid-America. Schooled in corridors of Catholic bone; drank blood briefly. Fermented in Ann Arbor; heavily indebted to U. Michigan. Chapbook 1985 by Clamor Press: *Poetry is a Form of Light*. Also in a few mags. Write to raise springboards for thought, sidestep rigidity. 'Who can dance a frozen man?' "

WILLIAM MAHER was born in San Francisco in 1950 "and spent most of my early years being called 'poor white trash' by the kids. My father was a cowboy, an artist, and a drunk. i hitchhiked a few times across america and spent most of the seventies doing the same in europe." He has co-written and performed in three independent features: *Lenz, Hero,* and *Cheatin Heart*. His poetry has appeared in *Beatitude, Compages,* and several Paris magazines.

DEVORAH MAJOR was born in California and raised in San Francisco. She is currently the statewide coordinator of California Poets-in-the-Schools. She was poet-in-residence at the African American Historical and Cultural Society for three years. Her work has appeared in *River Styx, Black Scholar, Zyzyva,* and *Y'Bird*.

PAUL MARIAH was born in 1937. He was the founder and has been the co-editor of ManRoot Books since 1969, the oldest gay press in America. His volumes include *Personae Non Gratae, The Spoon Ring,* and *This Light Will Spread: Selected Poems 1960-1975*. He co-translated, edited and published the *Complete Poems of Jean Genet* in 1981. He currently lives in Sonoma with his companion of 14 years. "No prizes. No awards. Just work."

JACK MARSHALL was born and raised in Brooklyn. He has worked as a long-shoreman, seaman, manager, cook, proofreader, housepainter and migrant farm laborer. He lived and traveled in Mexico and Europe before settling in San Francisco in 1968. His poetry titles are *The Darkest Continent, Bearings, Floats, Bits of Thirst,* and *Arriving On The Playing Fields Of Paradise,* which won the Bay Area Book Reviewers Award in 1984. A new book of poems, *Arabian Nights,* will appear in 1986. He has taught at several universities, including San Francisco State.

MARTIN MATZ's early Lorcan influences were transformed through his friendship with Pedro y Pedro and other South American shamans. He has spent over ten years traveling and living in Mexico, Colombia, Chile and Peru. His books include *Alleyways, No Magic Egypt Ever Blooms,* and *Time Waits: Selected Poems, 1956-1984.*

FRANCES MAYES teaches at San Francisco State University, and for three years was director of The Poetry Center there. She is the author of six books, including *Hours, The Arts of Fire, After Such Pleasures,* and *Sunday In Another Country.*

MICHAEL MAYO is the editor and publisher of this anthology. He was born in Syracuse, N.Y. in 1954. He lives and works in San Francisco.

MICHAEL McCLURE was born in Marysville, Kansas in 1932. His published work includes two books of essays, *Scratching the Beat Surface* and *Meat Science Essays;* two novels, *The Mad Cub* and *The Adept;* more than a dozen volumes of poetry, including *Ghost Tantras, September Blackberries, Star, Antechamber,* and *Fragments of Perseus;* and numerous plays, including *Josephine: The Mouse Singer,* which received the Obie for Best Play in 1978. He has traveled widely "to enlarge his vision of man in his various attempts to push away from his substrate."

DAVID MELNICK was born in Urbana, Illinois in 1938. He has lived in the Bay Area since 1963, with a few detours. His books include *Eclogs, PCOET,* and *Men in Aida, Book One.*

DAVID MELTZER was born in Rochester, New York in 1937 and moved to the Bay Area from Los Angeles in 1958. He is currently a member of the core faculty of the M.A. Poetics program at New College of California. He is the author of over 40 books of poetry, fiction, essays, children's tales and anthologies, the most recent of which are *Death: An Anthology of Ancient Texts, Songs, Prayers and Stories,* and *The Name: Selected Poetry 1973-1983.*

JACK MICHELINE is the author of thirteen books of poetry and prose. His play *East Bleeker* was produced at Cafe LaMama in NYC. Two one act plays have been produced in San Francisco. His books include *I Kiss Angels, Last House in America, North of Manhattan, Collected Poems, Ballads and Songs: 1954-1975,* and *Skinny Dynamite Stories.*

JANICE MIRIKITANI, third generation Japanese American, is Program Director of Glide Church/Urban Center. She has edited several anthologies, including *Third World Women* and *AYUMI, A Japanese American Anthology* spanning four generations. Her first book of poetry and prose was *Awake in the River*. The Pacific Asian American Women Bay Area Coalition and The Women's Foundation have both honored her achievements in art and social activism.

H. DAVID MOE was born in Corvalis, Oregon and has traveled extensively in the U.S., Cuba, Japan, Europe and Australia. He is an experimental poet and calls his personal aesthetic "Correctionism." For many years he edited and published the magazine *Love Lights*. His books include *Blindfolded Elephant, Plug In the Electric Dictionary, Immortal Amebas*, and *Oxymoron Nosedive Prayers*.

JOHN MUELLER was born in 1942, has lived in Asia and Europe, studied at the University of Vienna, and received his M.A. from The George Washington University. He has been the editor of FRAMMIS Magazine and has organized several popular reading series in San Francisco. His art work has appeared in several international journals and a number of group exhibitions. His books of poetry are *Venus, What Can I Say, Traces, Prussian Blue*, and *The Paramorphs*. He lives in Berkeley with his wife and child.

JAMES NOLAN is a native of New Orleans and has received both NEA and Fulbright grants. He has taught literature at Eckerd College and the Universities of Barcelona, Beijing and San Francisco. His two books of poems are *Why I Live in the Forest* and *What Moves Is Not the Wind*. He currently teaches at UC Santa Cruz.

HAROLD NORSE was born in NYC, and after attending schools and universities there, spent 15 years in self-exile wandering Europe, North Africa and the Near East. He returned in 1968 to live on the West Coast. His *Beat Hotel*, a surreal novella in the Cut-up method, is an underground classic. A revised and enlarged edition of *Carnivorous Saint*, which spans an unprecedented 45 years of gay poetry, will be published by The Crossing Press in late 1986. He is at work on his memoirs.

MICHAEL PALMER was born in NYC in 1943. After attending Harvard he lived in Europe, studying at the University of Florence. For the past several years he has worked as a choreographer with the Margaret Jenkins Dance Company. He is also on the faculty of Poetics at New College. His books include *Without Music, The Circular Gates, Notes for Echo Lake*, and *First Figure*.

PAT PARKER was born in Houston in 1944. She changed her college and her major when the head of the journalism department insisted "there's no place for Blacks in this field." Her five books of poetry include *Movement in Black* and *Jonestown & other madness*. She is currently the Director of the Oakland Feminist Women's Health Center. She lives in Pleasant Hill with her lover and two children.

JERRY RATCH was born in Chicago in 1944. He lives and works in Berkeley and is married to the artist Mary Ann Hayden, with whom he co-publishes Sombre

Reptiles Press. His eight books of poetry include *Puppet X, Clown Birth, Hot Weather: Poems Selected and New, Helen,* and his forthcoming *Lenin's Paintings,* from Illuminati. He has recently finished a series of 155 poems he calls "sonnets."

RICHARD RONAN was born and raised in industrial New Jersey. He graduated with his M.A. from UC Berkeley *summa cum laude.* He founded and taught an alternative high school for emotionally disturbed adolescents for 16 years in suburban New Jersey. His six books include *Narratives from America* and *A Radiance Like Wind or Water.* He lives in San Francisco, is preparing a manuscript of theater pieces, and is a professor of Ikenobo/Kebana.

EUGENE RUGGLES has been awarded grants from the National Institute of Arts and Letters and the NEA. His poems have appeared in *Poetry San Francisco, The Nation, The New Yorker,* and *Poetry.* His first book of poems was *The Lifeguard in the Snow.*

AARON SHURIN was born in Manhattan in 1947, and was educated at UC Berkeley and New College of California. His five books of poetry include *The Night Sun, Giving Up The Ghost,* and *The Graces.* His play, *Line Drawing,* was produced in 1979, and he has recently collaborated with dancer Joe Goode on a dance/theater piece, *Closer.* He lives and teaches in San Francisco.

RICHARD SILBERG was born in Brooklyn in 1942. He received his B.A. from Harvard College in 1965 and his M.A. in creative writing from San Francisco State in 1973. He is co-coordinator of the poetry series at Cody's Bookstore and associate editor of *Poetry Flash.* He lives in Berkeley and teaches writing at UC Extension and San Francisco State. His first book of poems was *Translucent Gears.*

STEVE SILBERMAN was born in 1957. "Conducted through tear gas clouds Wash., D.C. as a child by activist parents—read *Leaves of Grass* and *Howl* in high-school bed—apprenticeship w/Ginsberg Naropa Institute 1977 and Aaron Shurin 1984. I live in a noisy apartment in the Haight Ashbury w/companion John Birdsall, right now astonished by precise affectionately-detailed human lives in Williams' *Farmer's Daughters* stories."

JOHN OLIVER SIMON was born in New York in 1942 and has lived in Berkeley since 1964. One of his great-grandfathers was mayor of San Francisco in the 1870s, another owned the largest whorehouse on the Barbary Coast. His 14 books of poetry include *Roads to Dawn Lake, Rattlesnake Grass,* and *Confronting the Empire.* He works for the California Poets-in-the-Schools.

LESLIE SIMON was born and raised on the south side of Chicago. An instructor of Women's Studies at City College of San Francisco, she works other jobs to support her teaching and writing "habits." She has two children and is the author of three books of poetry: *Jazz/is for white girls too, i rise/you riz/we born,* and *High Desire.*

CAROL TARLEN is the associate editor for the short story magazine *Real Fiction*. She received her M.A. in creative writing from San Francisco State and is employed as a clerical worker at the University of California at San Francisco, where she is a member of the union there. Her short stories and poems have appeared in *Passaic Review, Ikon,* and *Sing Heavenly Muse*.

JULIA VINOGRAD was born in Berkeley in 1943. She received her B.A. in English from UC Berkeley and her M.F.A. from the University of Iowa. She has published over 20 chapbooks and two books of selected poems: *Berkeley Street Cannibals* and *Cannibal Consciousness*. Her collection, *The Book of Jerusalem,* was awarded a 1985 American Book Award.

ALICE WALKER won an American Book Award and the Pulitzer Prize for her novel, *The Color Purple*. Her other published work includes two collections of short stories, two novels, a volume of essays, a biography of Langston Hughes, and four volumes of poetry: *Once, Revolutionary Petunias, Good Night, Willie Lee, I'll See You in the Morning,* and *Horses Make a Landscape Look More Beautiful*. She was born in Eatonton, Georgia and lives in San Francisco.

A.D. WINANS was born in San Francisco and is the editor of Second Coming Press. In 1973 he received a PEN writer's grant and is currently on the board of directors of COSMEP, an association of independent book publishers. His books of poetry include *Straws of Sanity, North Beach Poems,* and *The Reagan Psalms*.

NELLIE WONG was born and raised in Oakland's Chinatown. A member of Radical Women and the Freedom Socialist Party, she was an organizer for the San Francisco Bay Area's Women Writers Union. Her first book of poems was *Dreams in Harrison Railroad Park*. West End Press will publish *The Death of Long Steam Lady* in 1986. She is also at work on a collection of prose and poetry, *Broad Shoulders*.

MERLE WOO is a socialist feminist lesbian, a lecturer at UC Berkeley, and a member of Radical Women and the Freedom Socialist Party. Her work has been published in *The Haight Ashbury Literary Journal, Plexus, Coming Up!, Alcatraz 3,* and *Breaking Silence, An Anthology of Contemporary Asian American Poets*.